# Eagles Are
# *Gathering*

*"An informed public is the key
to the preservation of liberty."*
—THOMAS JEFFERSON

## DEDICATION:

*My loving wife Susie, and our four daughters,
Larissa, Amanda, Michelle and Heidi.*

*And especially dedicated to America's middle class,
on whose ultimate fate the survival of the free world depends.*

Miller Family at West Point in 2006.

# Eagles Are
## *Gathering*

By Merlin Miller

Published by American Free Press
January 2016

# EAGLES ARE GATHERING

### By MERLIN MILLER

ISBN: 978-0-9881997-8-1

Published by:

AMERICAN FREE PRESS
16000 Trade Zone Avenue, Unit 406
Upper Marlboro, MD 20774-8789

### Ordering more copies:

Order more copies of *EAGLES ARE GATHERING* (softcover, 241 pages, $20 plus $4 S&H) from AMERICAN FREE PRESS, 16000 Trade Zone Avenue, Unit 406, Upper Marlboro, MD 20774. Call 1-888-699-6397 toll free to charge copies to Visa, MasterCard, AmEx or Discover. See more at www.AmericanFreePress.net.

### Subscriptions to AMERICAN FREE PRESS newspaper:

A subscription to AMERICAN FREE PRESS newspaper is $59 for one year (26 biweekly issues) and $99 for two years (52 biweekly issues) inside the U.S. Outside the U.S. prices vary. You can also order at www.AmericanFreePress.net. See a special subscription offer at the back of this volume or call toll free number above and ask for best current subscription offer.

### Reproduction Policy:

Material in this publication may be reproduced without prior permission in critical reviews and other papers if credit is given to author, full book title is listed and full contact information and subscription information are given for publisher as shown above.

(Cover Design and Political Artwork by David Dees—DDees.com)

# TABLE OF CONTENTS

GEORGE WASHINGTON

# *Treasonous Elements*

"Your love of liberty—your respect for the laws—
your habits of industry—and your practice of the
moral and religious obligations, are the strongest
claims to national and individual happiness."
—GEORGE WASHINGTON, 1789

AMERICA'S FOUNDING FATHERS had the courage and divine wisdom to create a nation unlike any in history. In so doing, they delivered a promise—for life, liberty and the pursuit of happiness. But America is sick and under attack. Not by any military, nor by God's hand, but by treasonous elements within.

The United States, the greatest nation ever conceived, is now on the precipice and needs her patriots to come to the rescue. She has been betrayed by self-serving politicians and a two-party system that no longer serves the American people, but instead serves special moneyed interests. America has also been betrayed by a controlled mainstream media that does not respect truth or righteousness, but instead promotes our social and moral decline. The global forces behind these betrayals are intent on destroying America, and sacrificing all that our forefathers built and that we hold dear—to establish, instead, a socialist New World Order in which they will surrepti-

tiously rule an unsuspecting yet increasingly enslaved mass—George Orwell's dark classic, *1984*, come to life. The evidence is clear to those who seek out truths, historic and current.

These global elites have debauched our currency, involved us in unjust and undeclared wars, opened our borders to massive Third World immigration, destroyed our production capabilities through government over-regulation and imbalanced trade agreements, and subverted our rights and constitutional protections. Government and the military-industrial-banking-pharmaceutical complex are America's only growth industries, and as the American middle class is being systematically wiped out, a totalitarian police state is evolving. The trusting and normally good-hearted American people have been deceived and gradually put to sleep, allowing for their systematic enslavement and inevitable despair. We have not been diligent, as our Founding Fathers admonished.

In the last 50 years, America's national character has been dramatically altered. The overwhelming white, Christian majority (90% in the mid-1960s) is now 65% and predicted to be a minority within the next 30 years. To question this ongoing immigration invasion, which is a radical demographic assault against America's core identity, or to question divisive and unconstitutional "affirmative action" programs is to be classified a "racist." To question Israel's excessive influence over America's foreign policy or the Jewish dominance in media and banking is to be classified an "anti-Semite." Our republic has been turned upside down, and Cultural Marxism and political correctness have silenced too many patriots for far too long.

America has traditionally been the beacon for the rest of the world, not a ruthless interventionist in the affairs of other nations, and it is time we restored our best traditions and America's reputation. The world should once again emulate us, not fear and despise us. This book is a call to arms—not for violence, but for an understanding of what ails America and how it came to be—and most importantly, what we must do to save her.

—MERLIN MILLER
January 2016

## ACKNOWLEDGEMENTS

# *So Many Virtuous People*

"Only a virtuous people are capable of freedom."
—BENJAMIN FRANKLIN

AT THE OUTSET, I WOULD LIKE TO THANK a genuine American patriot, Richard S. Thompson. I owe Dick my deepest gratitude, for without his passion and encouragement this journey would have never begun. Sadly, Dick was killed in a single car crash on June 10, 2007, as he returned from the 40th reunion for the surviving crew of the USS *Liberty*. Although foul play was not suspected, Dick's cell phone was never recovered, and he had told me of Israeli Mossad surveillance and inferred threats. Dick was a champion for the USS *Liberty*, spearheading their cause in many different ways. He had committed two days prior to his death, in front of several reunion attendees, that he would help secure funds for the motion picture production of their story (to become known as "False Flag"). It is a story which begs to be told—and which Hollywood and Israeli sympathizers have vowed to prevent. Thus far, they have succeeded.

My research path was lit by many and I hope that I accurately reflect their contributions along the way. For the most part, I will attempt to assimilate various findings and reference the work of others for the reader's further study.

I would like to especially thank those courageous journalists who report difficult truths in a world of increasing falsehoods. Specifically, the AMERICAN FREE PRESS (www.AmericanFreePress.net) and other publishers, editors, and writers who report factual history and honest, relevant news—rather than the propaganda and fluff which now pervade mainstream reporting. I would also like to thank and commend the internationally acclaimed, yet very politically incorrect David Dees (DDees.com) for his outstanding artwork, which is contained throughout this book.

There are many freedom events and I would like to commend Paul Topete and his band PokerFace (www.pokerface.com) for their bold activism in organizing the Freedompalooza event each of the last several years (freedompalooza.blogspot.com). I've been honored to be a part of this special gathering of truth tellers and liberty seekers.

Cadets drill at West Point Military Academy in New York.

I would also like to thank the United States Military Academy at West Point for the values that it imparts—with an appeal for the "Long Gray Line" to reevaluate what "Duty, Honor, and Country" mean. The Cadet Prayer encourages our future officers *"to choose the harder right instead of the easier wrong, and never to be content with a half-truth when the whole can be won."* My experiences have led me to have the greatest respect and admiration for our service members and their families. Their sacrifices can never be adequately acknowledged and I hope that future leaders find the strength to deploy them only in our nation's true defense. I would also like to honor America's Founding Fathers who, by God's grace and their unique wisdom and courage, gave this country its amazing start. The doctrines they inspired, and the documents they created and staked their lives for, including our Declaration of Independence, Constitution, and Bill of Rights, still represent our best hopes for the future.

I consider myself the most fortunate of men, a product of the American Dream. Like the clueless Forrest Gump, I've stumbled into some of the most incredible situations, and met the most incredible people—some famous, some infamous. I will include many in this book, as well as personal anecdotes that may surprise you, but I assure you are true.

—MERLIN MILLER
January 2016

WALT DISNEY

# CHAPTER 1

# *The American Dream*

"All our dreams can come true, if we have
the courage to pursue them."
—WALT DISNEY

⚜

BORN INTO POVERTY IN 1952, I was the middle of three children and, until I was six years old, we lived in a one-room house, without plumbing. As kids, we didn't know we were poor, sharing a corner bed and using an outhouse and hand water pump. We were happy and had a relatively normal youth. We didn't have a television, but my sister and I would go to our neighbors to watch "Zorro" or "The Mickey Mouse Club." In time, Walt Disney would become my idol and role model.

Near the end of WWII, my dad quit high school upon turning 17 and enlisted in the Army to fight the Nazis. When he left the service, he considered a boxing career, as he was undefeated for the Army in inter-service competitions, and later knocked out the Midwest Golden Glove champion in an exhibition bout. But while traveling through the Midwest, doing tree work, he met my mom at a boarding house where she lived and worked, and their lives took a fateful turn.

My parents were married much too young, but raised us to respect our German-Irish traditions and Christian values—and to love our country. Mom was only 16 when she became pregnant with my sister, and Dad was still a wild, young man—but he accepted his responsibilities and worked two jobs most of his life to improve the family's lot. They believed in the American Dream and knew that America's middle class offered a unique transit to a better life for anyone willing to work for it.

Miller Family in the mid-1950s.

Life was not easy, as both of my parents came from broken homes and neither graduated high school in the conventional sense, but obtained equivalency degrees later. I was the most fortunate, as I received a nomination to the United States Military Academy at West Point and became the first member of our family to graduate college. Both my sister and brother worked hard and did well serving in the Iowa National Guard. My sister jokes that military service was no challenge for us, since we grew up in a very disciplined home. Our parents passed away not long after retiring, but their lives were a classic example of the opportunities that a country like America could provide to ambitious, honest, and hard-working people.

With brother, Brian, and sister, Miriam, in late-1960s.

West Point opened up a world of opportunities for me, and my USMA class (1974) has been extremely successful, with numerous CEOs and General Officers, including four "4 Stars": Martin Dempsey (recently retired Chairman of the Joint Chiefs of Staff), David Petraeus (former CIA Director), Keith Alexander (former Director of the NSA and Cyber Command), and Walter Sharp. While at West Point, I met my future wife, Susie, and she has been my life's salvation. I enjoyed military service, but it was not my life's ambition and we left the Army in 1980.

June 5, 1974 Graduation at West Point.

December 28, 1974 saber wedding in Ocean City, New Jersey.

Motion picture producing had since become my goal, and after a three-year detour as an industrial engineering manager, I was accepted into the University of Southern California's "Peter Stark Motion Picture Producing Program." Susie was pregnant with our first child and we would have all four daughters while struggling to build my career in California. Learning, as I have since, how totally controlled and discriminatory the entertainment industry is against traditionally valued, Christian Americans, I should have chosen differently—but I was chasing the American Dream.

I can summarize by stating that a major portion of the problems now facing America are caused by a totally controlled and propagandizing mainstream media. There is a sinister agenda at work to destroy America from within and the mass media is its most powerful and insidious weapon—used to corrupt our beliefs, values, social norms, and governing political system. The American people know things are not right, but most do not understand how it has happened, who is behind it, or why.

My personal awakening and quest for truth began when I learned about the attack by Israel on the American spy ship, USS *Liberty*, while marketing the Western motion picture, "Jericho," in 2001-2002. I met Bob Scarborough, an independent cinema chain (Carmike) booking agent, and surviving *Liberty* crewman, who introduced me to their story. Strangely, as a military academy graduate, I had never heard of it, and therefore did not initially believe him. He directed me to Dick Thompson, which began a special friendship and my descent down the rabbit hole.

Thereafter, connecting historical facts with current intrigues, I migrated into politics and became a supporter of Congressman Ron Paul. He is a true statesman and courageous patriot, and his impact on America is still fomenting. In my opinion, his noble efforts will come to be historically regarded as the benchmark for the restoration of our republic. Unfortunately, he campaigned within a controlled two-party system and was media marginalized from any serious mainstream consideration—hence the great need for viable alternative parties and alternative media.

As we proceed, our efforts and the American Eagle Party will be mercilessly attacked—as isolationist, racist, and anti-Semitic. These false labels are constructed by global elites and their social engineers,

With Dr. Ron Paul at the 2008 Rally to Restore the Republic.

who control the public discourse to suppress truths, pitting various groups against each other. In combating their destructive agenda, we must fight to decentralize and limit government authority and the power of controlling special interests—to return freedom to the people. As concerned patriots, we cannot shrink from this "politically incorrect" effort to save our country and a future for our progeny.

We live in incredible times, which present extremely difficult challenges, but also life-enriching opportunities. America is now experiencing a new awakening and the existing world order will be turned upside down. Global power brokers and international bankers will try to retain their invisible grip on our lives and continue to destructively manipulate outcomes, but they will not succeed. The free exchange of ideas and truths, primarily through the Internet and talk radio, can no longer be contained and will forever alter their plans to enslave the bulk of mankind.

"Newsboy" is a small bronze sculpture by James N. Muir (www.jamesmuir.com).

# CHAPTER 2

# Down the Rabbit Hole

"Without Truth, Justice is lost,
and without Justice, Liberty is lost."
—JAMES N. MUIR

THINGS ARE VERY WRONG in the United States of America. Most citizens know it, yet they do not have a grasp on the severity of our situation. We, the most prosperous nation on Earth, are deeply in debt. The once most beloved country on Earth is now the most hated. Our economy lingers precariously while we conduct never-ending wars in Afghanistan and Iraq and threaten Iran, Syria, North Korea, and Russia, while supporting and fighting insurgencies everywhere. Our military personnel are exposed to in-creasing dangers and are being ma-nipulated and betrayed by forces within government that do not have the American people's best interests at heart. The foundations of this great nation are under assault in favor of a "New World Order" which ultimately seeks to destroy our na-tion's sovereignty and our individ-ual freedoms to create a global socialist entity hidden behind an il-lusion of democracy. This study will attempt to shine light on the forces which are behind this bizarre herd-ing of the masses, and why.

Among the public, trust in our political leaders (of both major political parties) is virtually non-existent. According to recent surveys, the percentage of Americans who say they trust the president, Congress, and judiciary is approximately 20%. We know that we have been lied to by our public servants and this trend continues, yet no one seems able or willing to do anything about it. A controlled and propagandist media is the principle barrier to gaining the truth and is increasingly the lead agent of our subversion. The family unit is fighting disintegration and our moral compass is under continual downward adjustment. Our education system is being hijacked away from local teachers and administrators and placed under the control of government bureaucrats, whose political dictates supersede the instructional priorities of school districts.

A pluralist society, such as America has become, can thrive with mutual respect and fairness. However when immigration laws create excessive social and economic upheaval and use of a common language is forsaken, we are setting the stage for racial and ethnic conflict and the demise of our nation. The Christian religion, which figured so prominently in our creation and growth, has been under relentless assault through judicial and legislative actions and media disparagement. Traditional and family-friendly institutions, such as the Boy Scouts, are continually on the defense against invasive and well-promoted advocacy for alternative lifestyles. Strange and relatively new biblical interpretations by evangelical leaders are disingenuously steering the Christian community to ardently support Zionism, thereby condemning Islam and any hopes for a just and lasting peace in the Middle East.

From a timeline perspective, it is increasingly plausible that an ongoing conspiracy of international oligarchs using activist organizations, the media, and political puppets as their principal agents, are behind many of history's destabilizing events and the problems we face today. Over the last century, anarchists, communists, fascists, and Zionists have ruthlessly promoted destructive agendas. Influential and often unwitting Jewish constituencies have been virtually hijacked to serve their needs, while other groups ignorantly acquiesce. To deny conspiracies is to deny human nature, and to dismiss the force of international financiers is to dismiss our current situation and the recordings of history. Unfortunately, where profit and power are at stake, human ruthlessness has no bounds and the global chess game can take on apocalyptic dimensions.

An informed people can neutralize the fears and trauma caused by these conspirators and their destructive acts. The republican system can work peacefully. We can take back our country, correct our course, and regain our liberties. But this can happen only if corrupting forces are harnessed and principled individuals light our way back to the path of humanitarian greatness.

Ironically, Winston Churchill once said, *"Men occasionally stumble over the truth, but most pick themselves up and hurry off as if nothing had happened."* We can no longer do that and expect to live as free people. It is time for heroes to wield the sword of truth, and journey where its enemies lie.

A Navy officer inspects damage to the USS *Liberty*.

# CHAPTER 3

# *The USS Liberty*

"Never before in the history of the United States Navy has a Navy Board of Inquiry ignored the testimony of American military eyewitnesses and taken, on faith, the word of their attackers."
—Dr. RICHARD KIEPFER, Captain, USN

FROM THAT CHANCE ENCOUNTER with a survivor from the USS *Liberty* I began to research one of the most bizarre yet true stories imaginable. The amazing survival of the USS *Liberty* with its crew of heroes is not generally known to the American public. The cover-up of that massacre is an incredible story in itself, but the *Liberty* injustice is merely the beginning of this story. Ironically, the ship's name took on special meaning as my research started to uncover increasingly shocking revelations about an extremely well-orchestrated and sinister assault on America's freedoms and traditional values.

On June 8, 1967, during the Six-Day War, Israel attacked the defenseless American ship, the USS *Liberty*, killing 34 crewmen and wounding 174 others. The *Liberty* was in international waters monitoring and transmitting signals received from the war zone. She was flying the American flag and her markings were clearly identifiable on that sunny day. Israel later claimed that the attack was an accident, a case of mistaken identity, yet several friendly overpasses by Israeli jets had preceded the attack and individuals familiar with the attack deny any legitimacy to Israel's claim.

Dr. Kiepfer, the ship's doctor, seriously wounded
himself, saved the lives of many *Liberty* crewmen.

A few published books offer details of the attack and speculation
about why it took place. *Conspiracy of Silence* was written by Anthony
Pearson, who had two articles about the USS *Liberty* previously published by *Penthouse* magazine. The magazine later regretted publishing the articles after enormous Zionist pressure. Pearson died
thereafter under mysterious circumstances while investigating another story critical of Israel.[1] James Ennes Jr., a surviving officer who
was on bridge duty at the time of the attack, published his account
in *Assault on the Liberty* shortly after Pearson. This was a brave effort
in that he defied instructions given to the crew (under threat of court
martial) to never disclose information about the attack. Those orders
were part of a conspiracy to cover up the true facts and allow the "incident," as it was called, to disappear from public scrutiny. Surviving
members of the crew were reassigned, with no two being assigned
together. This incredible cover-up was ordered by President Lyndon
Johnson, who on the day of the attack actually recalled Sixth Fleet
aircraft twice, after they had been dispatched to rescue the *Liberty*.

The ship's Captain, William McGonagle, who guided their survival
during the brutal attack, was awarded the Congressional Medal of
Honor. The *Liberty* is the most highly decorated ship, during an en-
gagement, in America's history, yet the American public knows nothing about it. McGonagle received his award at a Naval Shipyard, but
not from the president, who was pinning the same medal on a Vietnam hero that same day at the White House.

Capt. William McGonagle

During the prolonged and sustained attack by unmarked Mirage and Mystere jets, missiles, rockets, and napalm rained down on the ship. They were followed up by torpedo boats, which blew a 40-foot hole in the ship's side. The torpedo boats also fired at topside crewmen and destroyed life rafts as they were launched (a war crime). Two large helicopters with armed Israeli commandos hovered thereafter, but left, apparently in the belief that American naval forces were en route. It is truly amazing that the ship survived this relentless, nearly two-hour assault and is largely due to many individual acts of heroism. The first Israeli air assault wave destroyed all of the ship's antenna and communications equipment, and only due to the superhuman efforts of the many crewmen, including Terry Halbardier, who climbed the masts to string a new line, were eventual communications reestablished with the Sixth Fleet. This, perhaps more than any other act, contributed to their ultimate survival.

There has been much speculation about why Israel attacked the USS *Liberty*. Some suggest that Israel was committing war-crime atrocities against Egyptian forces and that *Liberty* intercepts might have revealed this, as well as the fact that Israel was the real aggressor in the war. Also, Israel was "cooking" communications by intercepting Egyptian, Jordanian, and Syrian messages and altering content before sending them on. This created deceptions about the actual progress of the war and encouraged their Arab enemies to reposition and blindly en-

James "Terry" Halbardier
—USS *Liberty* hero

gage troops, thus allowing Israel to expand their land conquests. There was also considerable pressure from other nations for a cease-fire. If the war were expanded, it would have enabled Israel to conquer the Golan Heights as well as consolidate their gains in the Sinai, Gaza, and West Bank. Peter Hounam's book, *Operation Cyanide*, postulates that the Six-Day War was actually planned and aided by the CIA and that the *Liberty* was to be sacrificed as part of an operation to bring the U.S. into the conflict, if necessary, and guarantee an overwhelming victory for Israel. Egypt, of course, would have been blamed for the attack—perhaps an echo of President Johnson's Gulf of Tonkin Incident, which escalated our involvement in Vietnam.

Hounam's book offers some disturbing conspiratorial aspects, especially considering the bizarre cover-up that followed. An excellent documentary video was produced for the BBC entitled "Dead in the Water," which Dick Thompson helped fund and produce. This documentary has continually been denied airings to American audiences due to pressure from pro-Israel groups.

In recent years, several other books have been written about the USS *Liberty*. The most poignant, in my opinion, is *What I Saw That Day* by surviving crewman Phil Tourney and his writing partner, Mark Glenn of "The Ugly Truth." The courageous Tourney currently hosts a radio program, "Your Voice Counts," on Republic Broadcasting Network. Also, *Attack on the Liberty* by James Scott, *Ship Without A Country* by Victor Thorn and Mark Glenn, and *Liberty Injustices* by Ernest Gallo are excellent accounts.

USS *Liberty* before and after the attack. What you can't see
is the 40-foot torpedo hole is below the water line.

Other books that offer insights into the *Liberty* attack are *Body of Secrets* by James Bamford, *They Dare to Speak Out* by former Congressman Paul Findley, and *The Zionist Connection II* by Alfred Lilienthal. Bamford offers an insider's expert analysis of the National Security Agency (NSA), the controlling organization for the *Liberty's* intelligence crew. Findley's book deals largely with the power of the American Jewish community to squelch any anti-Israel dissent, influence electoral outcomes, and determine American foreign policy. Lilienthal offers extraordinary insights into the Zionist movement, which has been so divisive among American Jews, and how it will never permit real peace in the Middle East. The greatest insights into the USS *Liberty* attack and cover-up can be obtained from the websites ussliberty.org, usslibertyveterans.org, and honorlibertyvets.org, which were constructed by surviving crewmen and their supporters.

Dick Thompson, 2nd from left, at the 2007 USS *Liberty* Arlington Memorial.

With Dick Thompson's sponsorship and tutelage, I attended some crew reunions and got to know these heroes and their personal stories. Eventually, I did write "False Flag," and although every effort has been made to deny its production, the screenplay can be read at http://MerlinMiller.com/False-Flag. Since then, an excellent documentary, "The Day Israel Attacked America," was produced and aired by Al Jazeera—however, without any promotion to U.S. mainstream audiences.

It is interesting to note that no formal congressional investigation has ever been made of the *Liberty* attack, despite repeated requests. Any congressperson or senator who has pressured for an investigation has been thwarted and in most cases defeated in the next election through the efforts of the American Israel Public Affairs Committee (AIPAC). This is the most powerful lobbying organization in Washington and is, in effect, the unregistered agent of a foreign government, which has and continues to foster Israeli spying against America.

Captain Ward Boston was the senior legal counsel for the Naval Court of Inquiry. In response to Israeli apologists who tried to claim that the attack was a case of "mistaken identity," he subsequently came forth with a declaration that clearly establishes Israeli culpability. In his declaration, he asserts that President Johnson and Secretary of Defense Robert McNamara ordered Admiral Isaac Kidd, President of the Court, to falsify the report. Both Admiral Kidd and Captain Boston were adamant in their conclusions that the attack was a deliberate effort to sink an American ship and murder its entire crew, but they followed orders.[2]

Secretary of State Dean Rusk, CIA Director Richard Helms, and later Chairman of the Joint Chiefs of Staff Admiral Thomas Moorer all held unwavering views that the attack was deliberate and, in effect, an act of war. The Court of Inquiry had only been given one week to make their findings, instead of six months, which they had recommended. During that short time they gathered a vast amount of evidence, including heartbreaking testimonies, but were not able to consider any of the more than 60 eyewitness accounts from those who were hospitalized. Select key testimonies that had been taken were later purged from the report. The board was also denied permission by Admiral John S. McCain, Jr., Commander-in-Chief, Naval

Forces Europe (and father of the Arizona senator), to travel to Israel to question any Israelis concerning the matter. Admiral McCain's chief legal counsel and later Judge Advocate General of the Navy, Admiral (Ret.) Merlin Staring, did not believe the evidence supported the report's conclusions but his review was terminated and the report sent to Washington, D.C. anyway with Admiral McCain's signature. My personal meetings with Admiral Staring revealed his frustrations.

Why is the case of the USS *Liberty* so important for our study? It marked a key moment in history, whereby the agents of a foreign country knew that they could control events within America. By controlling key elements of our media and political landscape, they knew that they could literally get away with murder. From the administration of Lyndon Johnson and thereafter, Zionist forces have clearly been in control of our Middle East foreign policy decisions. We thereafter became the principal benefactor for Israel and annually contribute billions of dollars to their military and civilian infrastructure. Under the Johnson administration, Israeli agents infiltrated American nuclear facilities and government oversight agencies, and stole nuclear technology and materials, enabling Israel's surreptitious, and to this day internationally unaccountable development of nuclear weapons. This has facilitated their hegemonic and warring ambitions in the Middle East.

How did we become the patrons of Zionism?

**ENDNOTES:**
1 *Operation Cyanide*, Peter Hounam, Vision Books, London, 2003, p. 125.
2 "Declaration of Ward Boston, Jr., Captain, JAGC, USN (Ret.)," Coronado, California, Jan 9, 2004.

DAVID BEN-GURION

# CHAPTER 4

# *Zionism & Palestine*

"We will expel the Arabs and take their place. In each attack a decisive blow should be struck resulting in the destruction of homes and the expulsion of the population."
—DAVID BEN-GURION, Israel's first prime minister

**Z**IONISM: Zionism has been defined as a plan or movement of the Jewish people to return from the Diaspora to Palestine. It is a movement originally aimed at the re-establishment of a Jewish national homeland and state in Palestine and now concerned with development of Israel.[1]

One hundred years ago, the American Jewish community was strongly opposed to the Zionist movement. They were assimilating successfully in America and did not support a plan to relocate the Jewish people to a partition of land in Palestine or elsewhere. Americans of the Jewish faith could freely practice their religion without fear of persecution and were developing a national loyalty to America. Conservative Judaism and Reform Judaism were growing as alternatives to Orthodox Judaism, which adhered to more extreme interpretations of the Talmud. The Jewish community was generally at peace and prospering in America.

Most religions, whether Christianity, Islam, Judaism, Hinduism, Buddhism, or Confucianism, express a spiritual belief and reverence for a superhuman power recognized as the creator and governor of the universe. Kahlil Gibran wrote, "In my thought there is only one universal religion, whose varied paths are but the fingers of the loving hand of the Supreme Being."[2] But extremist factions of each religion can employ their own perversions and create eternal conflict.

Israel Shahak's book *Jewish History—Jewish Religion* is a fantastic study of some of these historical perversions and how they have adversely affected the Jewish people and their ability to assimilate into host nations. Over 100 expulsions from various countries throughout history are testament to this challenge. Regarding the state of Israel, Shahak writes:

> There are two choices which face Israeli-Jewish society. It can become a fully closed and warlike ghetto, a Jewish Sparta, supported by the labour of Arab helots, kept in existence by its influence on the US political establishment and by threats to use its nuclear power, or it can try to become an open society. The second choice is dependent on a honest examination of its Jewish past, on the admission that Jewish chauvinism and exclusivism exist, and on a honest examination of the attitudes of Judaism towards the non-Jews.[3]

Shahak's assessment is honest and open, but would be repudiated by most Zionists and Orthodox Jews. Chief Sephardic Rabbi of Israel Ovadia Yosef, who was in coalition with Prime Minister Netanyahu and was honored with the largest funeral in his country's history, was quoted as having said, "The sole purpose of non-Jews is to serve Jews," comparing Gentiles to donkeys. To complicate things, since the late 1800s "Christian Dispensationalists" have been strangely interpreting the Bible to profess that Palestine would one day be given back to the Jews. British Prime Minister Benjamin Disraeli was a champion for the Zionist cause and, with the support of his friend Lionel Rothschild, advocated for a "restoration of Israel."[4] Edmond Rothschild would become known as the "Father of Israel" and the banking family would become their "royalty."

One of the early evangelical writers, William E. Blackstone, organized the first Zionist lobbying effort in 1891. He recruited J.P. Morgan, John D. Rockefeller, Charles B. Scribner and other financiers to underwrite a massive newspaper campaign for establishing a Jewish state in Palestine.[5] Today, the preachings of misguided but media-supported evangelical Christian Zionists have convinced the Christian community to support this campaign, and associated warring—

which is totally at odds with the Prince of Peace. This largely came about after publication of *Scofield's Reference Bible*. Cyrus Scofield, a forger, felon and trained lawyer, had been hired by the Rothschilds to write this dispensational reinterpretation of biblical events and Christian doctrine. Published by London's Oxford Press, it was given enormous promotion and incorporated into theology training and, with select clergy assistance, into Christian seminaries during the early 20th century.

Charles Carlson has produced an insightful video, entitled "Christian Zionism: The Tragedy and the Turning" (whtt.org), detailing this orchestrated subversion. Texe Marrs of the Power of Prophecy Ministries (powerofprophecy.com) has written many insightful books, produced informative videos, and hosted a weekly radio program contesting this hijacking and destruction of true Christianity. Not surprising to those who study this subversion, the term Judeo-Christianity, which first came into use in the 19th century, has sprung up like a new religion—perhaps designed to create a seeming bond when, in fact, the hyphen better represents their historic divergence.

Since earliest times, the quest for truth and the quest for power separated mankind. When Abraham received the calling 4,000 years ago and began to follow One God, man had to question if he would continue to hold pagan beliefs and honor many gods or believe in one supreme power. In the centuries that would follow, the twelve tribes of Israel came together with the conquest of Canaan. In time, the ten northern tribes of Israel would begin to assimilate with other peoples and, after the Assyrian conquest (8th century B.C.), would disperse throughout the world. In later centuries many would follow the teachings of Jesus and become a part of building the Western world. Others, who remained in the region, would largely become Islamic.

However, the southern tribe of Judah would follow a belief that God would accept them as the "Chosen Race," and they would ultimately dominate the rest of mankind. They believed they were chosen in this self-serving sense, rather than as emissaries to bring the word of "One God"—especially as promulgated through the Talmud from the Babylonian Captivity (6th century BC) onward. Inconsistencies in the Old Testament reflect these divergent postures.

By the time of Jesus, the Judaic Pharisees held internal power under the Roman Protectorate of Palestine. The Pharisees were threatened by Jesus's teachings of love, which challenged the materialism they inspired through fear and greed. By 70 A.D., when Jerusalem fell, the two remaining Judaic tribes were scattered and the struggle for man's soul took different directions. In the following centuries, Christianity would blossom with the teachings of the New Testament, and Islam would grow through the teachings of the Prophet Muhammad and the Qur'an. Judaism, based on its Mosaic Law (the Torah) and racist Talmudic interpretations, would often hold the Jewish community together by instilling a combination of fear and supremacy. Christian extremists would exacerbate this through religious persecutions. These interpretations and postures would create an ever-expanding gulf and resentments would grow, especially between Christians and Jews.

Judaists would often migrate as small groups, which grew into "ghettos," during the Middle Ages. The largest groups, which were of Semitic descent, would migrate across Northern Africa into Spain and be referred to as Sephardic Jews. Another group, which would grow to dominate the Jewish community, was called the Ashkenazi. It is primarily the Ashkenazi who would make up the largest percentage of European Jews, and those who migrated to America. Ironically, the Ashkenazi are not of Semitic descent, but were descended from the Khazars. According to Arthur Koestler's *The Thirteenth Tribe*, "the Khazar contribution to the genetic make-up of the Jews must be substantial, and in all likelihood dominant."[6] The Khazar kingdom converted to Judaism in the 8th century A.D., largely as a strategic move, since their Kingdom was located between the Black Sea and the Caspian Sea, wedged between the two growing super religions of Christianity and Islam. The Khazars had been a warlike and pagan people, and without this mass conversion, it is possible that the Judaic faith may have died out in the course of history. Over the next few hundred years, the Khazars would migrate into Russia and Eastern Europe, especially after the Mongol invasions.

It is ironic that today we refer to anyone who opposes things Jewish as "anti-Semitic," when in reality the majority of Jews are not a Semitic people. It is doubly ironic that the Palestinian and Arab peoples, who are Semitic and have been the victims of Zionist cruelties, are often accused of "anti-Semitism" for their resistance to Israeli land-grabs and oppression. A third irony is that the very name Israel was chosen for a Jewish state, when the ancient tribe of Judah rejected the more moderate beliefs of the ancient Israelis. Some scholars today believe this was done to cause confusion, to allow better acceptance of Zionist encroachments in Palestine.

### PALESTINE'S FUTURE

When one looks beyond mainstream U.S. media coverage and begins to discover the realities in Palestine, it is a shocking revelation. We, who have always prided ourselves on standing up for the little guy, are responsible for supporting the bully on the block, Israel. Most Jewish people are compassionate and would be very disturbed to know what is really going on in Palestine. They have undoubtedly been asked to contribute financially to Israel, and to support the political activities of various lobbyist organizations. If they only knew the truth of how they and the American public have been deceived, they would demand an immediate change to our foreign policy.

Courageous Israeli authors, Shlomo Sand (*The Invention of the Jewish People*) and Gilad Atzmon (*The Wandering Who?*) attacked the Jewish identity questions and their insights are causing reevaluation within Israel and Jewish communities throughout the world. In America, a brave journalist, Alison Weir, has created a website called ifamericansknew.com and has written an excellently documented, provocative book, *Against Our Better Judgment*, which contains startling facts about the situation in Israel/Palestine and the one-sided media portrayals that have exacerbated it. A great book, which reveals incredible information about the counterproductive Israel/U.S. relationship, is Jeff Gates's *Guilt By Association*. An excellent periodical publication which gives comprehensive and fair reporting to the sit-

Left, Alison Weir, shown next to a copy of her blockbuster book, *Against Our Better Judgment*.

uation is *The Washington Report on Middle East Affairs.*

The atrocities committed daily by the Israelis against the Palestinians are staggering. Palestinians are corralled like animals and prevented from free movement, even to their own lands and places of work. Separation barriers, gates, and fences restrict them from access to necessary services. Well-funded settlers move into Palestinian areas to claim their lands and possessions, not unlike the American settlers' dispossession of Native American populations.

The Palestinians are literally being starved into submission in an effort to ultimately drive them away. They cannot govern their own affairs, unless approved by Israel. The U.S. taxpayer pays for these oppressions and for the military weaponry that subjugates the Palestinian people. When desperate youths fight back, they are labeled as terrorists. Irrational suicide bombings are virtually all that we hear about in the U.S. mainstream media. Ms. Weir has startling facts on how unfair and disproportionate the reporting actually is—with only a small percentage of Israeli "abuses" reported against a very high percentage of Palestinian acts of "terrorism." Part of this is a result of the Associated Press and other international or state news agencies having their offices located in Israel, or screened by a pro-Israeli editor prior to general distribution.

Rachel Corrie

It is amazing that hardly anyone even knows about Rachel Corrie, the young American girl who was killed by an Israeli bulldozer as she tried to defend the home of a Palestinian family. Where is the appropriate and fair media coverage and why is there no outcry from our political leadership? Even when former President Jimmy Carter wrote *Palestine: Peace, Not Apartheid* he was castigated by Israel-firsters and had to apologize before his grandson could gain any support to effectively run for a Georgia state seat.

During the 2010 Gaza Flotilla, Ken O'Keefe, a former Marine and Gulf War veteran, was aboard the *MV Mavi Marmara,* trying to bring aid to the suffering Palestinians. As a truth, justice and peace champion, Ken lessened the carnage of the Israeli attack on the ship by helping to disarm two Israeli commandos. He suffered while subsequently incarcerated but eventually was allowed to leave—as, fortunately, many alternative media sources monitored the situation. Ken is unorthodox... but a hero in my mind. We got to know each other while attending conferences in Iran. After returning from one trip, I was asked by an FBI agent what I thought of him. My response, "There's no one I'd rather have watching my back." The agent's re-

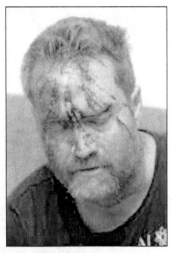

Ken O'Keefe

action (a former Marine, himself) was curious to me, and I suspected that he held a grudging respect beneath his conditioned attitude of condemnation.

While America was engaged in the trumped up wars against Iraq and Afghanistan, and now during the civil strife in Syria and Ukraine, Israel continues to covertly support terrorist groups, including ISIS, fomenting discord throughout the Middle East. They kill Palestinian resisters and innocent bystanders and incarcerate thousands without charges or due process. They attack Lebanon at will and threaten to attack Iran if it continues to develop nuclear capabilities. The U.S. and Israel feel that they can deny nuclear capabilities to others, even for peaceful purposes. Meanwhile, Israel defies all international calls for inspection of its nuclear weapons program and refuses to join the nuclear non-proliferation treaty.

In 1986, Mordechai Vanunu, a former Israeli nuclear technician, in opposition to weapons of mass destruction, revealed Israel's nuclear weapons program to the world. He was subsequently lured to Italy by a female Mossad agent, drugged, abducted, and transported to Israel, where he was convicted behind closed doors. He spent 18 years in prison (11 in solitary confinement) where he suffered cruel and barbaric treatment. Vanunu has since been restricted and rearrested several times, and has suggested that his treatment was as a result of converting from Judaism to Christianity.[7]

MORDECHAI VANUNU

Humanitarian rights organizations are continually condemning Israel, while the American public is blinded by media smokescreens, and unknowingly continues to support Israel's racist and inhumane actions. However, despite these smokescreens and disinformation campaigns, increasing numbers of people are becoming aware of the tragic reality. Most admirably, courageous anti-Zionist Jews have stepped forward to reveal these difficult truths. They include Dr. Norman Finkelstein, Henry Makow, and the colorful Brother Nathanael.

From left to right: Dr. Norman Finkelstein (NormanFinkelstein.com); Henry Makow (HenryMakow.com); and Brother Nathanael (BrotherNathanaelChannel.com).

For Israel's own best long-term interests and to advance the prospects for peace in the Middle East, a fair and just solution must be pursued with the Palestinians.

CHAPTER NOTES:

1 *The American Heritage Dictionary*, Houghton, Mifflin Company.

2 *Spiritual Sayings of Kahlil Gibran*, Bantam Books, April 1970, p. 113.

3 *Jewish History—Jewish Religion*, Israel Shahak, 1993, p. 13.

4 "Tracking the Roots of Zionism and Imperial Russophobia," Laurent Guyenot, VeteransNewsNow.com, February 13, 2015.

5 Bud Fleisher, Democrats.org

6 *The Thirteenth Tribe*, Arthur Koestler, Random House, New York, 1976, p. 180.

7 "Mordechai Vanunu," Wikipedia.

Donald James, aka Thomas Dresden.

# CHAPTER 5

# *Conspiracies*

"When a well-packaged web of lies has been sold gradually to the masses over generations, the truth will seem
utterly preposterous and its speaker a raving lunatic."
—THOMAS DRESDEN [DONALD JAMES]

Many conspiracy theories have evolved over the centuries
in response to history's cataclysmic events. These most
often originate in response to the actions of secret
groups, some with ancient occult origins, believed to be
operating for financial gain and power. The Illuminati and other
groups, some associated with Freemasonry, have often been accused
of organizing and implementing mass dissentions. With the leaders
at the top often protected from
the actions at the bottom, these
organizations have been very effective and through a system of
establishing various levels of secret initiation are hidden from
any general awareness, even by
their own membership (which
believe they are supporting noble
causes).

President and Mrs. Kennedy arrive
in Dallas on Nov. 22, 1963.

President Kennedy ad-
dressed this in a speech which can be viewed on YouTube and which
some speculate may have been a contributing factor to his early
death.

President Kennedy said:

The very word secrecy is repugnant in a free and open society, and we are as a people inherently and historically opposed to secret societies, secret oaths, and to secret proceed-
ings. But we are opposed around the world, by a monolithic
and ruthless conspiracy, that relies primarily on covet means
for expanding its sphere of influence, on infiltration instead
of invasion, on subversion instead of elections, on intimidation instead of free choice.

It is a system that has conscripted vast human and material
resources into the building of a tightly knit, highly efficient
machine that combines military, diplomatic, intelligence, economic, scientific and political operations. Its preparations are
concealed, not published. Its mistakes are buried, not head-
lined. Its dissenters silenced, not praised. No expenditure is
questioned. No secret is revealed.

That is why the Athenian lawmaker, Solon, declared it a
crime for any citizen to shrink from controversy. I am asking
for your help in the tremendous task of informing and alert-
ing the American people. Confident with your help, man will
be what he was born to be, free and independent.

From the French Revolution until the early 20th century, conspiracies most often took the form of undermining Catholicism in Europe and orchestrating the overthrow of monarchs through anarchy.
Many books have been written which contain overwhelming evidence in support of these conspiracy theories.

Some of the most thought-provoking books include *The Controversy of Zion* by Douglas Reed, *Secret Societies and Subversive Movements*
by Nesta Webster, and *The Secret World Government* by Count Cherep-
Spiridovich. Reed's perspective is particularly revealing in that he was
a world-renowned journalist during the first half of the 20th century.
His career seemingly died overnight, when he began to write of happenings from a historical perspective.

The power of these conspiratorial movements grew substantially
in conjunction with the growth of Zionism in the late-1800s and
early-1900s. Their ruthlessness was most obvious during the Russian
Revolution when Bolsheviks led the overthrow of the Czar and
brought that country to despair through civil war and the barbaric

imposition of communism. Unknown to many people, American banker Jacob Schiff, aligned with the Rothschild family, was a major backer of the Bolsheviks.

Many theories relate to international financiers controlling the political arena through economic leveraging—most effectively begun with the deceptions and deeds of Amschel Mayer (who changed the family name to Rothschild).

> "Permit me to issue and control the money of a nation, and I care not who makes its laws."
> —AMSCHEL MAYER ROTHSCHILD

During the 19th century, the Rothschild clan and associates were notorious for funding conflicts between nations and gaining power, if not control, through manipulations of key members of the various governments. Despite the best intentions of many government servants, the human factor can easily intercede, and the general public's best interests can be betrayed. As George Washington said, "Few men have virtue to withstand the highest bidder."

To relate this to current times, one only has to read *Confessions of an Economic Hit Man* by John Perkins. It is clear how corruption has grown from an individual and familial level to the organized subjugation of nations. The leverages imposed by ruthless individuals and companies, wealthy governments, and through such organizations as the World Bank, International Monetary Fund, and the United Nations are incredible. The financial tools for empire building have certainly not served the best interests of American citizens, but have padded the coffers of certain business interests and leveraged for a one-world economy by exploiting the human vices of representatives of target nations.

> "We shall have World Government, whether or not we like it. The only question is whether World Government will be achieved by conquest or consent."
> —JAMES PAUL WARBURG[1]

Unfortunately, the American Jewish community has been manipulated over the last century by a number of influencers to support a Zionist agenda, which serves internationalists' designs. A climate of fear has been developed throughout the ages and perpetuated in their communities through Talmudic indoctrination. Kevin McDonald, in his study, *The Culture of Critique*, writes "Intense hatred of perceived enemies appears to be an important psychological characteristic of Jews."[2] Nesta Webster, in *Secret Societies and Subversive Movements*, observed, "In reality nothing is more cruel than to encourage in the minds of a nervous race the idea of persecution; true kindness to the Jews would consist in urging them to throw off memories of past martyrdom and to enter healthfully into the enjoyment of their present blessings."[3]

Jewish fears are very real, however, and history has shown varying levels of persecution throughout the ages, the most significant in recent times being Nazi persecutions before and during WWII. While there is no doubt that the Jews were persecuted during Hitler's reign, there is also an ongoing reevaluation of events and many revisionist historians are increasingly questioning the origins and extent of the Holocaust. The case of Ernst Zundel is of particular interest. He was a Canadian publisher of German origin, who published *Did Six Million Really Die?* He was subsequently accused and prosecuted under an old "false news" clause (determined to be unconstitutional years later). The two trials, which took place in Canada in the 1980s, received scant and one-sided press in the U.S. but raised serious concerns for free speech.

Robert Lenski's *The Holocaust On Trial* is a most startling account of the trials. In it, many expert witnesses refute the accuracy of earlier findings, thus casting serious doubts on the truthfulness and extent of generally accepted accounts of the Holocaust and on the fairness and conduct of the Nuremberg trials.[4] We should in no way minimize the horrors of that era, but we should also be careful that falsifications and exaggerations are not promulgated to benefit certain groups and disadvantage others. Particularly disturbing is the increasing loss of individual freedom that has resulted by restricting or disallowing historical inquiry. Truth does not fear investigation, yet in Europe thousands of people have been fined or incarcerated for merely questioning the growing inconsistencies of the Holocaust story. Why? Enormous sums of reparation payments have funded the nation of Israel and any loss of validity to these claims could endanger Israel's future and increase public scrutiny over their own oppressive actions.

One German judge, in sentencing a Holocaust "denier," went so far as to declare that "truth is no defense." I twice visited Ernst Zundel in the Mannheim, German prison in which he was incarcerated for five years. This was after he had been kidnapped from his home and wife in Tennessee (on tenuous visa violations), to then spend two years in solitary confinement in Canada, before being extradited in the middle of the night back to Germany. He seemed an intelligent,

Ernst Zundel

peace-seeking man, unfairly victimized by his pursuit of historic truths.

Zionist leaders often use a combination of fear and "chosen race" supremacy to mobilize the Jewish population and apply pressures where needed to promote the Zionist agenda. This is most apparent today through the vast network of organizations (such as the Anti-Defamation League and Southern Poverty Law Center) that are always on the lookout for potential threats and working to promote Zionist interests, often while subordinating America's best interests. When threats are thus perceived, their networks are activated to fight and destroy it—even when the threat was unfairly perceived or is an unjust business or political maneuver. These individuals, as "sayanim," are called upon to give their aid to any call for protecting Zionist interests. This is sometimes employed by the Israeli Mossad. While these servants may sometimes be considered traitorous in their actions against America, they are considered loyal to their Israeli brethren and that is their first priority.

A most recent example is the case of Jonathan Pollard, who was released in 2015 from a "life" prison sentence for stealing and selling top-secret information to the Israelis, who shared it with others. Hundreds of U.S. intelligence operatives were compromised, many losing their lives, and American intelligence operations were irreparably damaged. Pollard's release was due to persistent Israeli pressures and was most likely granted as a form of appeasement, along with substantial increases in aid to Israel. This appeasement has not stopped Israeli sabotage of U.S. foreign policy actions, as is apparent by

Spy for Israel Jonathan Pollard

AIPAC's ongoing efforts to scuttle the Iranian nuclear agreement. Pollard is to be greeted with a hero's welcome in Israel, a nation which offers sanctuary to those who have committed crimes in other nations.

Alfred Lilienthal, in his thorough analysis *The Zionist Connection II: What Price Peace?* makes the disturbing observation that Americans of the Jewish faith increasingly give their first loyalty to the state of Israel over that of the U.S. Many American Jews are made to feel guilty for not choosing to migrate to their "homeland" of Israel. To compensate, they donate large sums of money and apply significant pressure on American politicians to sanctify Israel, increase foreign aid to Israel, and shield Israel from any scrutiny.[5]

Incredibly, prolific Hollywood producer Arnon Milchan (with 130 features), whose net worth is over $5 billion, has publically admitted that he served as an arms dealer and spy for Israel, providing technology and materials for their nuclear program and supervising government-backed bank accounts and front companies.[6] He was recruited by Israeli President Shimon Perez, who indicated that "his strength is in making connections at the highest levels." Milchan is still walking free and being honored by Hollywood's elite. His last two films, "12 Years a Slave" and "Birdman," won as best picture at the last two Academy Awards.[7] Why wasn't he condemned and arrested, instead? His films (including "Natural Born Killers") are sometimes detestable to traditional American audiences, but his impact on societal beliefs and values cannot be underestimated. He was also executive producer of "JFK," a successful misinformation effort,

Arnon Milchan is flanked by (left) Shimon Perez and (right) Benjamin Netanyahu.

which totally shielded Israel from any culpability. I suggest reading the late Michael Collins Piper's account of the Kennedy assassination, *Final Judgment*, and Laurent Guyenot's keen analysis at www.veteransnewsnow.com.

In my opinion, Zionism is being used as an enabler for a grand New World Order scheme, and continued service to the symbiotic designs of their internationalist brethren places long-term Jewish interests in peril.

### CHAPTER NOTES:

1 Before U.S. Senate Committee on Foreign Relations, Feb 17, 1950. [James Paul Warburg (1896-1969) was son of Paul Moritz Warburg, nephew of Felix Warburg and of Jacob Schiff, both of Kuhn, Loeb & Co., which poured millions into the Russian Revolution through James's brother Max, banker to the German government, Chairman of the CFR].

2 *The Culture of Critique*, Kevin McDonald, 1st Books Library, 2002, p. 14.

3 *Secret Societies & Subversive Movements*, Nesta H. Webster, A & B Books Publishers, reprinted 1994, p. 381.

4 *The Holocaust on Trial*, Robert Lenski, Reporter Press, 1990.

5 *The Zionist Connection II*, Alfred M. Lilienthal, ps. 743-747.

6 "Arnon Milchan Reveals Past as Israeli Spy," *The Guardian*, Nov 26, 2013.

7 Arnon Milchan, Wikipedia.

J. EDGAR HOOVER

# CHAPTER 6

# PNAC & 9/11

"The individual is handicapped by coming face to
face with a conspiracy so monstrous he cannot believe
it exists. The American mind simply has not come to the
realization of the evil which has been introduced into
our midst. It rejects even the assumption that human
creatures could espouse a philosophy which must ultimately destroy all that is good and decent."

—J. EDGAR HOOVER

The Project for the New American Century (PNAC) was the
work of ruthless disciples of political philosopher Leo
Strauss. Founded by William Kristol and Robert Kagan,
PNAC members include Dick Cheney, Jeb Bush, Donald
Rumsfeld, Paul Wolfowitz, Richard Perle, Scooter Libby, Elliot
Abrams, John Bolton, William Bennett, Richard Armitage, and a long
list of Zionist/New World Order advocates. Originating as a neocon
think tank, PNAC issued a document in 2000 calling for the radical
restructuring of U.S. government policies, involving military expan-
sionism and centralization of power. This process of transformation
could not be effected under the watchful eye of patriotic Americans
". . . absent some catastrophic and catalyzing event—like a new Pearl
Harbor."[1] These fanatics, many of whom are dual Israeli citizens, were
closely aligned with multinational corporate interests and the defense industry. They advocate for an elitist New World Order to be
created from the ashes of a sacrificial American empire. By early 2001,
many were administration officials or advisors with an uncanny link-

age to the events of 9/11, which were about to unfold.

Life in America, and throughout much of the world, changed forever on that day. Our responses were not based on research of the facts, but due to a controlled and prepackaged media barrage and restrictive channeling of the investigation. With the Patriot Act, our rights were literally suspended. Not only have the America people's longstanding liberties been violated, but we have attacked other nations without rational congressional oversight, on the basis of lies. Iraq had no weapons of mass destruction nor connection to 9/11. Bin Laden, who had previously worked for the CIA (as Tim Osman), denied any involvement in 9/11, was never indicted, and was suffering from kidney failure, reportedly dying in December of 2001.[2]

The truths about the events of 9/11 have been withheld from the

Key PNAC Members clockwise from upper left: Dick Cheney, Jeb Bush, Donald Rumsfeld, Paul Wolfowitz, Eliot Cohen, John Bolton, Lewis "Scooter" Libby.

# WHO IS TO BLAME FOR THE IRAQ WAR?

Left to right: Row one—Albert Wohlstetter, Oded Yinon, Richard Perle, William Kristol, Robert Kagan. Row two—David Wurmser, Paul Wolfowitz, Joe Lieberman, William Safire, Eliot Cohen. Row three—David Frum, Norman Podhoretz, Kenneth Adelman, Charles Krauthammer, Benjamin Netanyahu. Row four—Philip Zelikow, Elliott Abrams, Lewis "Scooter" Libby, Douglas Feith, Bernard Lewis.

American people. The growing evidence, much of it circumstantial, has been falsely labeled as "conspiracy theory" by the corporate media and the government, which many believe are complicit in a massive cover-up. Many questions remain unanswered as government "conclusions" are increasingly and vehemently disputed by reputable scientists, engineers, pilots, emergency responders, etc. Reasonable inquiries have been consistently subverted and diligent investigators marginalized. Increasingly, though, reliable Internet sources, foreign presses, and foreign intelligence services and leaders have proclaimed that 9/11 was a Mossad/CIA operation designed to begin the "War on Terror" and increase US/Israeli hegemony in the Middle East. Since then, other polarizing international events, which should demand serious scrutiny, have been used to foster a war-mongering dialogue. If these conspiracies prove to be true, then our government has been clearly taken over from within—and treason, of the highest degree, has been committed and is being covered up.

The public was never given the facts about Building 7 (which collapsed at freefall speed without being hit by any aircraft). The mainstream media avoids it, as did the 9/11 Commission. The dancing Israeli's (who videotaped and celebrated the WTC attack) were whisked back to Israel where they reported on TV that they had been sent to document the event.[3] Our military defenses were conveniently undergoing exercises, simulating a similar attack, and not responding as they should have. Dick Cheney, commanding from a bunker, insured that. Israelis in the World Trade Center were warned to leave two hours before the attack. Months before, warnings from "Able Danger" and other sources were ignored and loyal agents, such as John O'Neill, who had been chief investigator of Osama Bin Laden, conveniently died on 9/11 as the newly hired head of security at the World Trade Centers for Kroll Associates. The World Trade Center security companies, the highly insured new owner of the buildings, the companies providing security for the airports where the hijacked aircraft originated, and the coordinating investigative teams—all had strong interests in a neocon agenda to reshape the Middle East and engineer conflict between the Christian and Muslim worlds to the benefit of Israel.

Over 2,300 architects and engineers have gone on record disputing the "official" version of 9/11, along with thousands of law enforcement, military, fire and safety personnel, pilots and flight attendants, and foreign and domestic intelligence operatives. The physical evidence was immediately removed and shipped to China, in violation of investigative protocol. The criminal and/or subverting elements within our government (who controlled the investigative processes) must be identified and removed, so that a real and thorough investigation of the events of 9/11 can commence.

When studying the illogical and damaging actions of many of the key players in positions of authority, such as Michael Chertoff, the prospects of conspiracy take on greater significance. Chertoff, as head of the Criminal Division of the Justice Department, and whose father was a rabbi and mother was a Mossad agent, oversaw the unconscionable release of WTC material evidence and suspect Israeli detainees. Later, as Secretary of Homeland Security, in conjunction with other dual citizens he controlled access to evidence and corralled dissent. Subsequently, he profited from the sale of airport scanners, while restricting Americans' rights.

Among the many credible websites that challenge the official narrative are ReDiscover911.com, WhoDidIt.org, 911JusticeCampaign.org, and Reinvestigate911.org. James Corbett's popular and cynical "9/11: A Conspiracy," a video he described as "Everything you ever wanted

Michael Chertoff

to know about the 9/11 conspiracy theory in under five minutes," can be seen on YouTube, as well as numerous other 9/11 videos. They and many professionally detailed books are gaining in public acceptance as more people become aware of the serious discrepancies in the 9/11 narrative. Perhaps the most comprehensive newspaper coverage has been supplied by *American Free Press*. Dr. Alan Sabrosky, former Director of Studies at the U.S. Army War College, also gives courageous and convincing testimony indicting Israel on YouTube and through veterans' publications for which he writes.[4] Lastly, a short and factual enumeration of the key events and players can be found at http://wikispooks.com/wiki/9-11/Israel_did_it.

Larry Silverstein, who acquired the World Trade Center Complex just prior to 9/11 and is close friends with Benjamin Netanyahu, profited from the destruction.

In this study, we will not go into great detail on these events and the trail of lies and subterfuge that has blinded the American people to support Israeli/Zionist actions via their orchestrated "War on Terror." Keep in mind that 9/11 was a catalyzing event, which has led to large-scale conflicts, a redefining of our way of life, and, potentially, the ultimate destruction of life on Earth through the pitting of Christians against Muslims. The 19 Saudi dupes were not the real perpetrators of 9/11 (as Lee Harvey Oswald was not the killer of JFK), and increasing numbers of people in the military and security services know it. A wonderfully insightful book at connecting the intrigues which resulted in America's hijacking is Laurent Guyenot's *JFK-9/11: 50 Years of Deep State*. Also, Rebekah Roth has written the insightful fiction novels *Methodical Illusion* and *Methodical Deception*, which uniquely explore the facts of 9/11 from a flight attendant's perspective.

My own research and travels of the last several years, concerning issues related to our foreign policy (indirectly resulting from 9/11), brought me to the attention of Homeland Security—which, in my opinion, serves as a protector for these dark forces that have hijacked and still control America. Unfortunately, our best people are being used in service to these usurpers and betrayers. Fortunately, they are

increasingly becoming aware of this bizarre reality. We must do our best to aid their uncomfortable "connecting of dots." Although the facts are not yet complete, a rational person would conclude that the circumstantial evidence, indicting Israel and its neocon accomplices, is overwhelming and demands a real and thorough investigation.

Washington's recent and devastating military operations in the Middle East following 9/11 have made the United States a pariah in the world—

Rebekah Roth, author of *Methodical Illusion* and *Methodical Deception*.

as well as sacrificing our treasure and the blood of our young people, while disregarding individual liberties at home. We must find the courage and honesty to root out corruption and evil at all levels. This will not be an easy process, but is one that is most necessary.

In response to an FBI agent's query as to whether I thought justice would soon be restored to our country, I said, "We'll get our country back when the Silversteins come under indictment."

**CHAPTER NOTES:**
1 *9/11 Hard Facts.*
2 Egyptian news AL-WAFD, December 26, 2001 (also reported by Fox News).
3 Israeli television.
4 VeteransNewsNow.com.

*"Rightful liberty is unobstructed action according to our will within limits drawn around us by the equal rights of others. I do not add 'within the limits of the law' because law is often but the tyrant's will, and always so when it violates the rights of the individual."* —THOMAS JEFFERSON

# CHAPTER 7

# Controlling Politics

"Behind the ostensible government sits enthroned an invisible government owing no allegiance and acknowledging no responsibility to the people. To destroy this invisible government, to befoul the unholy alliance between corrupt business and corrupt politics is the first task of the statesmanship of today."  —TEDDY ROOSEVELT

~

Political corruption would rise to new dimensions with the election of Woodrow Wilson and creation of the Federal Reserve System (Fed) and IRS. Wilson was elected due to a split in the Republican Party when Theodore Roosevelt was induced to run against the incumbent Taft. The bankers were firmly reestablishing themselves, and determining to never let go.

"This Act (the Federal Reserve Act, Dec 23rd, 1913) establishes the most gigantic trust on earth. When the President (Woodrow Wilson) signs the Bill, the invisible government of the Monetary Power will be legalized... The worst legislative crime of the ages is perpetrated by this banking and currency Bill." —CONGRESSMAN CHARLES A. LINDBERG, SR.

Also in 1913, the number of congressional representatives became set, which was never the intention of our Founding Fathers. This has arbitrarily reduced the true representation of the people and enabled "special interest" domination over Congress. (See http://thirty-thousand.org for an amazing analysis.)

President Wilson was an easily influenced scholar (bribed through an extramarital affair) and his career and decisions were largely made by Edward Mandell House, referred to as Colonel House (although he was not a military man). According to *The Controversy of Zion* by Douglas Reed, "Mr. House did not guide American State policy, but deflected it towards Zionism, the support of the world-revolution, and the promotion of the world-government ambition."[1] In addition to Colonel House, President Wilson's three other most trusted advisers were all Zionists: Mr. Bernard Baruch, Mr. Louis D. Brandeis, and Rabbi Stephen Wise. They, along with Zionism's international emissary and eventual first Israeli president, Chaim Weizmann, were able to manipulate Wilson to enter WWI on the side of England, although American sentiment more closely supported Germany. This action was a payment to England made by international Jewry. In return, England would support Zionist ambitions to establish a Jewish state in Palestine. The leveraging document was "The Balfour Declaration." Thereafter, America would gradually take the baton from England and become the primary patron of Zionism.

When Germany realized how they had been sold out by the European Jewish community to bring America into the war, they were resentful and these sentiments, along with the unconscionable injustices of the Treaty of Versailles and international banker funding of the communist movement, led to conditions that brought Hitler to power. Hitler wanted to extricate Germany of the Jews and was actually working with the Zionists to this end. The Zionists saw, through a totalitarian state, better prospects for creating conditions that would force the migration of European Jews to Palestine—an action necessary for the Zionist dream to unfold.

According to Benjamin Freedman, a wealthy and influential American business man, who was privy to meetings of American and international Zionist leaders, "*The Zionists and their co-religionists everywhere, are determined that they are going to again use the United States to help them permanently retain Palestine as their foothold for their world government.*" Freedman, who converted from Judaism to Christianity, gave a speech at the Willard Hotel in 1961 (available on YouTube), which offered incredible insights into how we were manipulated into WWI and WWII and how through Zionism we will be sacrificed into WWIII to serve their aims.[2]

During the early 1920s a disturbing document was published called "The Protocols of the Learned Elders of Zion." First published in 1905, it was supposedly a record of meetings of Zionist leaders held in the late 1800s. In detail, it is a ruthless plan for the subjugation of humankind to a controlling Zionist kingdom. Whoever the authors were, they were brilliant, and evil, with a keen understanding of the dark side of human nature. The Jewish community condemned it as a forgery, while it became a blueprint for the history of the 20th century. Concerned leaders in the 1920s called for its study and Henry Ford published a series of articles in his *Dearborn Free Press* calling for the study of *The International Jew*.[3] In England, Lord Northcliffe published a series of articles and attempted further study of "the Jewish question." Douglas Reed offers firsthand insights into the troubles that then befell Lord Northcliffe, leading to his bizarre death.[4]

Benjamin Freedman

Meanwhile in the Middle East, the former lands of the Ottoman Empire had been carved up in accordance with the Sykes-Picot agreement. The Balfour Declaration had not been honored, as its difficulties became apparent and the British (and French) had also made land promises to Arab leaders during WWI. The lands encompassing Palestine by the early 1920s were overwhelmingly Arab with a minority of Christians and a very small Judaic population. The Zionists realized that the only way to fulfill their vision was to have a mass influx of Jews from around the world migrate to Palestine. This process was encouraged, many lands were purchased and the Jewish population grew but still remained a small minority. WWII and the selling of the Holocaust would change that. The greatest victors coming out of WWII were the Zionists; they would not only benefit from enormous (and still ongoing) war reparations from Germany, but they also built a strong case for the need of the Jewish state to accommodate the misplaced Jews of Europe.

Following the war, most European Jews would have preferred to remain in or return to their host lands, but were not given this option. Also, pressure from the Zionists greatly reduced the number of immigrants that would be permitted to enter the U.S. or Great Britain. The Zionists leveraged to force a large and desperate body of Jews to migrate to Palestine. By this time, they had succeeded in converting much of the American Jewish community to support the migration and the establishment of an Israeli state. To give insight into the mindset of the Zionist leaders, David Ben-Gurion, future prime minister of Israel, was quoted, "If I knew that it was possible to save all the children of Germany by transporting them to England, and only half by transferring them to the Land of Israel, I would choose the latter, for before us lies not only the numbers of these children but the historical reckoning of the people of Israel."[5]

By 1946, acts of Zionist terrorism were directed against the British in Palestine who by that time wanted to extricate themselves from the messy situation. When the "Israeli War for Independence" began in 1948, Zionists ruthlessly terrorized the inhabitants of Palestinian villages to force them to leave and fear return. President Harry Truman, with strong Zionist support in America, immediately recognized the new state of Israel. At about the same time, Stalin began his purges of the Jewish communist leadership in Russia, causing American leaders to condemn the Soviets and call for the immigration of Russian Jews to Israel—heating up the "Cold War." As America and Western Europe united in opposition to the spread of communism, Zionists would increasingly abandon their open affiliations with communism and become aligned with "republican" forms of government.

Prior to the 1948 Israeli War for Independence and Palestinian flight, referred to as "Nakba" (the catastrophe) by its Arab inhabitants, the UN was looking to carve up Palestine and grant to a new state of Israel up to 55% of the lands of Palestine, even though their numbers by this time could only justify about one-third of a land assignment. As a result of the War, Israel would actually come to hold approximately 78% of Palestine. The remaining 22% would be acquired as "Occupied Territory" during the Six-Day War of 1967, as well as the Golan Heights portion of Syria.[6]

As Alfred Lilienthal described, *"Ignorant, misled Americans insisted on judging the Middle East conflict in terms of the survival of refugees from Hitler, never as the Zionist building of a nation that required expulsion of the overwhelming majority of the Palestinian people from their country, along with expropriation of their lands, homes and property."*[7] Since then, the state of Israel has passed numerous racist laws, directly discriminating against its Arab inhabitants and refugees, trying to get them to leave and never return. Israel's Arab neighbors have rallied in opposition and there has been no real peace in the region since. It has often been proclaimed that the U.S. has only one friend in the Middle East, implying Israel, but General George S. Brown responded best: "Before Israel, America had no enemies in the Middle East."

By the early 1960s, Israel needed something to sustain her existence. She was not getting enough new immigrants to insure a Jewish majority and her economy was dependent on external support. Prime Ministers David Ben-Gurion and later Golda Meir wanted nuclear weaponry, control of the river headlands, and Israel's security interests to be adopted by the United States. President Kennedy, although a supporter of Israel, wanted to halt the arms race and present a face of fairness in the Middle East. He wanted America to maintain good relations with other nations in the region and to pursue just solutions for the Palestinian refugee problem. Stephen Green's book, *Taking Sides*, gives great political insights into this.[8]

President Kennedy offered $600 million to build a nuclear-powered desalinization plant in Israel if the state would stop construction of its nuclear reactor at Dimona and not try to control the waters of its neighbors, but Israel refused.[9] Kennedy continued to try to delineate between U.S. and Israeli national interests and pushed for a humanitarian solution to the Palestinian problem. However, U.S. sponsorship for a UN resolution to go before the General Assembly was sabotaged by the assassination of the American president.[10] Kennedy's successor, Lyndon Johnson, would turn out to be a loyal supporter of Israeli interests and the next few years would bring incredible successes to their collaborations, culminating with the Six-Day War. Lyndon Johnson would go on to provide covert support for Israel's development of nuclear energy and weaponry, and would bring the U.S. to the verge of WWIII by supporting Israeli plans and execution of the Six-Day War.

One of the CIA's chief plotters, James Jesus Angleton, helped Israel for years and was later honored with two monuments in Israel.[11] Angleton would subsequently be dismissed from the CIA by Director

John F. Kennedy (right) restrains Lyndon Johnson.

James Colby, who although an excellent swimmer, would mysteriously die by drowning in four feet of Chesapeake water. It was this same Angleton who in earlier years tried to steer the CIA investigations of the death of President Kennedy toward the Soviets. The Warren Commission Report ultimately and ridiculously labeled Lee Harvey Oswald as the lone assassin (supported by Arlen Specter's "magic bullet" theory). Unfortunately, Oswald was killed at the hands of terminally ill bar owner Jack Rubinstein before any other information could be revealed. In addition to Kennedy's scrutiny of Israeli actions, it is also believed that the president intended to disempower the Federal Reserve System, restoring issuance authority of the currency to the U.S. Treasury, such that it would eventually not be subject to Federal Reserve charges of interest. President Kennedy, who was also working to end our involvement in Vietnam, had begun acting as a true president, concerned foremost with the interests of America. His assassination was the turning point in modern American history, and the beginning of our decline and subservience to Zion and its ensuing New World Order.

The nuclear gates literally unlocked during the Johnson administration and during those years U.S. aid to Israel would grow exponentially. This would also be a time of increasing UN condemnation of Israeli actions, yet unquestioning U.S. support. The U.S. position on the UN Security Council assured no viable action would ever be taken against repeated Israeli aggressions and oppressions against the Palestinians and their neighbors. It is amazing that any country could so arrogantly defy so many UN resolutions of condemnation and be supported by only one nation—the supposed vanguard of freedom and justice, America.

Johnson would also spearhead immigration reform, which would allow for the influx of literally tens of millions of Third World refugees over the next few decades. Unchecked immigration has been one of the greatest destroyers of the otherwise nearly invincible American nation.

Since President Johnson, other presidents have been less enthusiastic in their praise of Israel, but all have shown a disproportionate level of support. However, President Richard Nixon covertly challenged Jewish influence in America. In private discussion with Reverend Billy Graham, he expressed concern for their control of the media. President Nixon also requested officials in his administration to investigate the high numbers of Jewish employees in certain government agencies.[12] I've met some of the concerned individuals who were caught in this Machiavellian power contest. Not surprisingly,

Nixon's political career quickly ended with the Watergate conspiracy, a cover-up action that pales in comparison to the disturbing executive actions of other presidents.

Our two major political parties may advocate different domestic and foreign policies, but both have become increasing and unquestioning supporters of Israel. As Ariel Sharon was quoted, *"Don't worry about American pressure on Israel. We, the Jewish people, control America, and the Americans know it."* Politicians seem to compete in lavishing praise, especially since that praise is usually rewarded by special interest support at election time and favorable media coverage. This coverage can make or break a political career overnight, against seemingly impossible odds.

An excellent example is the campaign, ultimately successful, to unseat popular Congresswoman Cynthia McKinney of Georgia. Her sin? She would not sign an affidavit of unwavering support for Israel, which would have essentially obligated her to AIPAC's political dictates. Their money then poured into opposition coffers, and unrelenting media attacks began. As an ethical political activist, this courageous woman continues to fight for the American people, in defiance of the corrupting influences of AIPAC and other lobbies, which unfortunately hold the overwhelming majority of Congress hostage

Cynthia McKinney

> "And if after having elected their man or group, obedience is not rendered to the Jewish control, then you speedily hear of 'scandals' and 'investigations' and 'impeachments' for the removal of the disobedient." —HENRY FORD

Moneyed special interests now select the candidates and a mainstream media, which they own and control, elects them. The Federal Elections Commission has even expressed their helplessness in preventing this "buying of candidates" due to congressional finance rules that allow for unlimited PAC funding. Like racehorses, candidates are groomed and paraded before us. Their billionaire owners, such as Sheldon Adelson, George Soros, the Koch brothers, Haim Saban, Norman Braman, and others consider it their right to control America's political process. Disturbingly, they are also staunch Israel-firsters and war enthusiasts.

What are the odds that two families (Bush and Clinton), with questionable qualifications, could occupy the office of the President of the United States for 20 consecutive years (not to mention George

H. Bush's eight years as vice president)? This almost increased to 28 years as Zionist supporter and media darling Hillary Clinton pre-pared for 2008. Her unpopularity with a large segment of the popu-lation and the strange emergence of Barack Obama gave the puppet masters an alternative, which they could sell through the media to the gullible American public—especially since John McCain repre-sented absolutely no change to the previous eight years of Republi-can/neocon warmongering.

President Obama has since proven to be the Marxist that his shal-low record would indicate, and racial and immigrant conflicts are now being orchestrated to accelerate America's social and economic decline. Hillary subsequently filled a key role in the ongoing global-ization effort, as a dishonest and inept secretary of state, and now as the Democratic frontrunner. Establishment candidate Jeb Bush could still possibly lead the Republican ticket, as the presidential contest stage for 2016 is being predetermined by the puppet masters. America was not conceived as a republic to be ruled by onerous family dy-nasties who serve global elites and not the American people.

Under Obama, America has continued its suicidal empire building. While we maintain military bases throughout the world, oil and terrorism remain the transparent issues, but the underlying issue of world domination should not be disregarded, as Zionists plan the next stage of their New World Order through the social and economic destruction and stratification of America, and preparations for more war.

Already, America is quickly approaching the status of a "police state." Since the events of 9/11 and implementation of the Patriot Act, we are progressively losing our constitutional rights. Clerics have been advised to submit their flocks to government authority in the event of any civil unrest, and repeated attempts are being made to

emaciate our First and Second Amendment rights. Possession of firearms is the constitutional right of all of our citizenry to prevent government from becoming tyrannical. It was never to define the type of weapons permitted for hunting, yet efforts are ongoing to severely limit our gun rights. This campaign is never ending by political elitists, such as Diane Feinstein. Unbelievably, she stated before the Senate Judiciary Committee, "All vets are mentally ill in some way and government should prevent them from owning firearms." If we have any trepidation, it should be for "foreigners," who have no compassion for the rights of American citizens, but are being recruited into our armed forces and security services.

It should also be of interest that America's top "policemen," especially during the critical period following 9/11, included dual Israeli-American citizens Michael Chertoff (Director of Homeland Security) and Michael Mukasey (Attorney General). And in keeping with Washington's political fealty to Israel, President Obama's first Chief of Staff, Rahm Emanuel, was also an Israeli citizen. As reported in *Washington Jewish Week* (Dec. 4, 2008), an overwhelming number were to be tapped for his administration, including his national security team. Ira Foreman, executive director of the National Jewish Democratic Council, noted that "because Jews dominate every aspect of American government, it is not unusual that Jews dominate the Obama transition

team and will dominate the Obama Administration." It is unfathomable to me that this is allowed, as dual-citizen loyalties for another nation are a clear and serious threat to our security.

**CHAPTER NOTES:**

1 *The Controversy of Zion*, Douglas Reed, Veritas Publishing, p. 232.

2 Benjamin H. Freeman's speech given in 1961 at the Willard Hotel in Washington, D.C. on behalf of Conde McGinley's newspaper, *Common Sense*.

3 *The International Jew*, Henry Ford Sr., reprinted 1995 by CPA Publisher.

4 Reed, pp. 295-299.

5 David Ben-Gurion, quoted from translation of Shabtai Teveth's *Ben-Gurion*, pp. 855-856.

6 www.ifamericansknew.com

7 Lilienthal, p. 106.

8 *Taking Sides*, Stephen Green, William Morrow & Company, 1984.

9 *The Secret War Against the Jews*, John Loftis and Mark Aarons, St Martins Press, 1994, p. 260.

10 Green, pp. 183-186.

11 Hounam, p. 229.

12 Loftis and Aarons, p. 309.

DWIGHT D. EISENHOWER

# CHAPTER 8

# National Defense

"In the councils of government, we must guard against the acquisition of unwarranted influence, whether sought or unsought, by the military-industrial complex. The potential for the disastrous rise of misplaced power exists, and will persist." —DWIGHT D. EISENHOWER

The United States government's most important duty, besides preserving constitutional freedoms for its people, is to safeguard the nation from external threat. However, this should not involve policing the world or providing for the defense of other nations. Nor should the military be used in support of the ambitions of multinational corporations—but only for the defense of vital American interests. We should not engage military forces unless war is justified and declared by Congress. However, it appears that more war, not diplomacy, is in our future. See Mike Whitney's July 3, 2015 "The Pentagon's '2015 Strategy' for Ruling the World" at counterpunch.org.

Currently, American military forces are spread throughout the world, protecting other nations at great peril to our service people and at great financial cost to the American taxpayer. According to the Stockholm International Peace Research Institute, U.S. defense expenditures remain 45% higher than just before 9/11 and exceed that of the next seven nations, combined! Through the "War on Terror," we have been placed on a permanent war footing. Military promotion is only a part of the equation. Subsequent service in defense industries can be quite lucrative, especially to those who have facilitated the promotion of

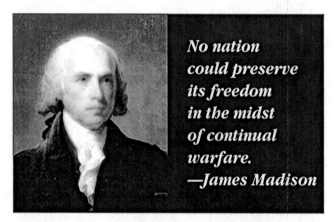

*No nation could preserve its freedom in the midst of continual warfare.*
—James Madison

huge defense contracts, which have been booming.

America's standing military should be significantly reduced, to be supplemented in times of need by well-trained "state and local militias." Our people should never be denied their constitutionally protected right to keep and bear arms. Instead, they should be encouraged and prepared to defend their homes, families and country from real threats, as militias were intended.

Currently, while Washington is supposedly involved in its never-ending "War on Terror," U.S. borders have been left unprotected. The U.S. is undergoing an invasion of illegal immigrants, which poses a significant danger to our internal security as well as great costs to the American people. Our borders should be secured immediately by the military, if necessary, and maintained as required. However, in accordance with the Posse Comitatus Act, military forces should never be directed against U.S. citizens.

Regarding the "War on Terror," the odds of a terrorist attack striking any individual American is extremely remote. Statistically, you are more likely to be struck by lightning or drown in your own bathtub. Accordingly, the costly and oppressive Homeland Security Department and the TSA should be immediately disbanded. The "Patriot Act" (and its successor "Freedom Act") is the most misnamed piece of legislation in U.S. history. It removes the right of habeas corpus, which is the fundamental right for an accused to challenge his accuser face-to-face. Worse is that the Patriot Act violates the 1st, 4th, 5th, 6th, 7th, 8th, 9th, and 10th Amendments to our Constitution!

In December of 2011, by a vote of the 93 to 7, the Senate passed the National Defense Appropriations Act (NDAA) which allows for the indefinite detention of American citizens and eliminates the Posse Comitatus Act—which was passed by Congress after the Civil War to prevent the use of federal military and National Guard for the enforcement of laws against its own citizens. Unfortunately, our representatives are in league with powerful interests who profit from war. Congresspersons and senators advocate for companies that service the war machine and provide lucrative employment in their districts and states.

The Patriot/Freedom Acts, NDAA, and equivalent infringements on liberty should be immediately repealed. America is not a dictatorship, nor an empire—and as Benjamin Franklin said, *"Those who would give up essential liberty to purchase a little temporary safety deserve neither liberty nor safety."*

Future foreign deployments should be limited to operations and occupations of strategic importance and only when properly authorized. We must, however, maintain our forces in an advanced state of readiness with an adequate research and development budget. We must also honor obligations to our service personnel, insuring that veterans receive proper care and earned entitlements.

The U.S. should, in no way, share its technologies and operational plans with other nations. And regardless of any other consideration, America cannot financially continue its presently chartered course of military aggression.

To protect against manipulations, U.S. intelligence services should not allow foreign nationals or their special interests to infiltrate American defense institutions and government agencies. U.S. military and intelligence services should restore real security to America by protecting our borders from legitimate threat, while protecting American citizen rights.

We should implement America First policies to strengthen our national defense, while restoring America's reputation in the world as a fair arbiter for peace.

## OUR MILITARY

Vietnam is probably the first example in our nation's history when the military did not have the patriotic support of our civilian populace. The war was unpopular because we had enacted the draft, our involvement lacked a clear, just cause, and the military was denied resources to quickly win it. On the news each night, we could witness the horrors of war while the costs in human lives and to our economy mounted. Vietnam only benefited certain business interests and was a great diversion from the more important challenges facing America.

There are many parallels between Vietnam and Iraq and Afghanistan, unjust wars in which the U.S. should never have been involved. None of these wars were in America's best interests, and the military, in both cases, was faced with a dilemma: do they loyally support a civilian leadership, which has clearly shown that it does not have the nation's or the servicepersons' best interests in mind, or do they stand up in protest?

One of the worst presidents in our nation's history was Lyndon Johnson. Not only was he ruthless and self-serving, but he was disloyal to our troops and would not listen to advice from the military leadership. It was a time when generals did not have the conviction to stand up for what was right. Colonel H. R. McMaster's *Dereliction of Duty* is an excellent study on this. Due to the military draft, the war became increasingly unpopular with the public and eventually led to its end—once the warmongers' game wore thin. Today, Vietnam is a trading partner... and their workers have replaced American workers in industry.

Since we do not currently have a draft, our military has been better supported in the Iraq and Afghanistan campaigns than it was in Vietnam, and we have had better popular support for our troops. However, the wars themselves have been disingenuously engineered for the profit of banking and corporate interests, while sacrificing America's national interests. If we truly wish to support our troops, we should demand that our politicians end these unjust and undeclared wars, and return our forces stateside. As a republic, we should not be trying to police the world for globalist interests. *Base Nation: How U.S. Military Bases Harm America and the World*, by David Vine, lays out the dangers of American military dominance and the enormous and often hidden costs.

Military personnel are taught to never question orders unless obviously illegal. In the case of political deceits, illegality is never easy to ascertain and not within the realm of a soldier's expertise or duty. During Vietnam, had the generals, who were in the know, stood up to President Johnson's deceits and abuses and resigned in protest, the outcome of our involvement may have been much different. By resigning or retiring from military service, a soldier is no longer obligated to silence, and when they know of serious transgressions by our leadership, they should speak up. Unfortunately, President Bush signed an executive order, no doubt unconstitutional, forbidding government employees from whistle blowing. Thankfully, several senior officers at least expressed their opposition to our campaign in Iraq and to the poor leadership of Secretary of Defense Donald Rumsfeld, eventually resulting in his replacement.

When looking through history, we can observe a recruitment of "warrior elites" for service to the political class. In my lifetime, such notables as Dwight D. Eisenhower, Alexander Haig, Wesley Clark, and David Petraeus have been groomed for high political office. I have come to personally know many military officers who have served as CEOs of major companies, who have headed U.S. agencies and departments, chaired major political parties and controlled large investment groups and foundations. Most are wonderful, hardworking people, who consider themselves patriots. Some have considered supporting the themes of this book, including alternative media ventures, only to be steered away due to political correctness and their relationships and vulnerabilities within the power structure.

Of great importance to America's restoration is the next tier of military leadership, colonels and generals, who are wooed by the financial overlords of Wall Street and defense contractors. It is reported that 80% of three- and four-star generals take lucrative consulting or executive positions upon retirement. General Ray Odierno, known for controversial statements and tactics, strangely signed on with JP Morgan.[1] Is the banking industry preparing for war against the people and another Sherman's March?

**CHAPTER NOTE:**
1 "The Pentagon Door Revolves Again," Philippe Gastonne, TheDailyBell.com, August 25, 2015.

HENRY KISSINGER

# CHAPTER 9

# The Long Gray Line

"Military men are dumb, stupid animals to be used as pawns for foreign policy." —HENRY KISSINGER (Perhaps proving his point, Kissinger received the Sylvanus Thayer award from West Point)

I joined the Long Gray Line on July 1, 1970. I'm still not sure how I made it in. I'd broken my left arm playing football before the physical exams of the previous year, but fortunately, it healed in time. The earlier written exams were more difficult, since I was left-handed and the cast forced me to be a righty. I somehow became an alternate candidate from Iowa, having applied because a military reservist uncle had recommended it to my parents. This was during the height of Vietnam and some politicians, in defiance to the war, were not nominating candidates. As a result, my congressman, Neal Smith, got a last-minute additional slot. I had been a wrestler in high school and fortunately won my match the day before I met my congressman. I always wanted to believe that it may have influenced him.

What a shock it was to join over 1300 new cadets as we entered "Beast Barracks" and a demanding new life. Attrition brought us down to a little over 800 by graduation day on June 5th, 1974. The Class of "74 is probably the most infamous of recent decades, and I got to know an incredible group of young men—many of whom went on to great success in the military, industry, and business. Women weren't to arrive at the academies until two years after our graduation. While there, we went through many challenges together and formed bonds that would last forever. We still meet and correspond regularly. The lessons imparted were the best one could ever experience and I am forever grateful for the intellectual, physical, and moral development.

The first two years we attended mandatory religious services, but legal challenges forced the academies to abandon that requirement. However, at the start of my second year, I met my future wife, Susan, who was just beginning at nearby Ladycliffe College, a girls' Catholic school. She brought sunshine to gray skies. We regularly attended mass, giving direction to a guy who avoided church like the plague (having been lost between the Protestant and Catholic backgrounds of my parents). Unfortunately, Ladycliffe has since closed, due to hard times for parochial colleges, and has been converted into West Point's welcome center, museum, and visiting officer billets. It lies just outside West Point's main Thayer Gate, in Highland Falls, NY.

With Susie at West Point

West Point is actually America's longest continuously garrisoned post and was selected as the site for our nation's military academy due to its strategic location on a bend of the Hudson River. George Washington, who led our Revolutionary Army, was the strongest advocate for a military academy. He knew the importance of having a professionally trained officer corps to lead our forces. In my opinion, Washington was our greatest hero, with a humble devotion to doing right. However, he and others were concerned that we not establish a large standing army, and that they be under the control of civilian leadership. The strategy was to maintain local militias, with an armed citizenry to call upon during times of threat. Thomas Jefferson was initially opposed to the formation of the academy, but later changed his mind, recognizing the need for a well-trained officer corps. As our nation's third president, he commissioned the academy in 1802.

America's greatest—Washington and Jefferson.

Our current senior officer corps, composed largely of West Pointers, has served our nation with the highest distinction through two Iraq wars and other campaigns. Other former officers now occupy high posts in various agencies of our government and in industry. We do have capable leadership and hopefully they will increasingly stand up for "America first" interests and exert a true patriotic influence on a political landscape, which has been treasonously misshapen by neocon influencers and their enablers.

I have observed troubling instances of West Point graduates serving the Zionist/New World Order agenda, largely due to propaganda and manipulations. Some profit from the growth of government and service to it, or to multi-national corporations, and thus remain impervious to the problems faced by most citizens. Although many are aware that America is drifting away from its noble ideals, they remain ignorant of the evils that their unquestioning subservience is creating. Ultimately, they will not be shielded from the ramifications and if they themselves do not suffer, their progeny will. Fortunately, some are coming to this realization.

I'm often asked about some of our more famous classmates, including Martin Dempsey, David Petraeus, and Keith Alexander. They have been quite successful for their leadership abilities, but also because they have faithfully served a political establishment that, in my opinion, doesn't always protect our country's best interests.

Immediately after graduation, four of us volunteered to serve with the Iowa National Guard for a month. Marty Dempsey joined Colen Willis, Joe Greer and myself. I have clear memory of surveying via helicopter the incredible damage done to Ankeny, Iowa as a result of a devastating tornado. Marty has quietly (except for his famous "Irish singing and limericks") risen through the ranks as a consummate professional. He had to walk an incredibly fine line as Chairman of the Joints Chiefs of Staff. In this political position, he advised the president and answered to various Senate and House committees. As our nation's highest-ranking officer he oversaw all of our military operations, and was under great pressure from the military-industrial complex, warmongering politicians and even foreign interests—many of which want to continually expand the wars. I believe that Marty helped to keep us from escalating unwarranted conflicts, and was a voice for sanity—keeping the neocon chickenhawks from totally sacrificing America's military to their war profiteering plans.

With USMA Classmate, General (Ret.) Martin Dempsey.

David Petraeus is intelligent, personable, and very competitive. At West Point, he excelled as an academic "star man" and athlete. David also married the superintendent's lovely daughter, Holly Knowlton. As one of our shining stars, I believe he was being groomed for high office and was regularly promoted by the national media. His successes were largely in service to the neocon/Zionist political and media establishment.

In December of 2009, I sent David a treatise that connected military, political, and media intrigues—challenging many of the orthodoxies. David is conscientious and, along with other influences, I believe began to question the Middle East situation from the perspective of what was truly best for America. In March of 2010, he publicly addressed the Israeli/Palestinian situation as being potentially endangering to our troops. Stating this truth was a political faux pas and David came under heavy neocon criticism. He did his best to mend those fences, but became a bit concerning to the Zionist establishment, which he had so faithfully served.

They needed to keep him on their farm, and hence I believe Paula Broadwell (nee Kranz), who had spent time on an Israeli Kibbutz, was embedded to write his story. I find it unusual under those "wartime" circumstances that this attractive biographer, who didn't have major publication experience, was sent to join him for a lengthy period of time in Afghanistan. At any rate, their drama unfolded in such a way as to keep David captive. Today, he works for Kohlberg, Kravis, Roberts (KKR) and is rolled out to advocate for American exceptionalism, globalism, and fealty to Israel—under the guidance of neocons and the banking establishment. I suspect his probation, and compensations, will keep him on their farm for at least the next two years. It is unfortunate, as David might otherwise have made a good president.

Many believe that he was simply a victim of his own ambitions and indiscretions. I rather believe that he was a prime target for ruthless Zionist manipulators, and they have further plans for him. In mid-2013, I probed to see if he might consider outreach to Iran for peace and understanding. He declined on the basis of having been CIA director and not allowed for a post period of two years to involve himself in international diplomacy efforts. Unfortunately, it did not prevent his controllers from sending him, and other military icons, to the next two annual Bilderberg meetings, far from the watchful eye of the American public. Bilderberg is an international elitist assembly that meets in private luxury to develop plans and set objectives through their influence and control of international finance, politics and media. Bilderberg and Rockefeller supported sister organizations, the Council on Foreign Relations (CFR) and the Trilateral Commission bring influential leaders together under the tutelage of the "Global Elites."

Keith Alexander held a less visible, but equally powerful position as Director of the National Security Agency (NSA) and Head of the Cyber Command. At a class function in August 2011, I approached Keith to ask him about the USS *Liberty*. He indicated that he knew about it, but then hedged. Strangely, I looked about and there was a 15-foot radius around Keith, his wife, and me—with no one else in it. For a jam-packed room, this meant that we hadn't used deodorant, or others didn't want to be perceived as listening in on what might have become a contentious discussion. Keith retired after Edward Snowden's revelations about NSA spying on Americans, and Keith's discomforting responses to constitutional probes. Personally, I firmly disagree with his interpretations of our Constitution, specifically the 4th Amendment. I understand that Keith went to work for banking interests upon retirement, providing cybersecurity services for compensations that would make kings blush.

Although most of my classmates are respectful of studied analysis, some have been thoroughly brainwashed, rejecting any critique of American exceptionalism or our military escapades. Nearly all would be in agreement with my concerns, if they knew the truths. Military people want to believe that the country respects their sacrifices. They want to feel good about their service, as most joined for patriotic reasons. However, our civilian leadership has betrayed the military, using and abusing them for multinational corporate and banking schemes, and not for the true defense of the American people.

With Delta Force legend, Lee Van Arsdale, the "real deal."

I compare the current Academy divisions with those that occurred during the Civil War, when Southern and Northern brothers were pitted against each other. Then, it was a banker-engineered economic division, erupting as states' rights vs federal power (the Southerners were on the right side of the Constitution). Today, it is nationalism vs globalism. We took oaths to the U.S. Constitution, not to international bodies. However, lies and manipulations are impelling us to support global missions for the benefit of bankers and their vast network of beneficiaries. The Navy has even developed slick ads, professing to be a "Global force for good." It is time for our military, and especially our Academy grads, to reevaluate these perpetual war missions, to once again serve the American people, rather than international elitists.

What we need is a "Veterans League of Honor (VLH)"... focused on former military personnel doing right (opposing drones, torture, unjust/undeclared wars) and standing for truths, regardless of how difficult. This group is much needed as an organization and ethical guide. At West Point, our motto is "Duty, Honor, Country." Today, unfortunately, Duty is being defined by treasonous forces, and Country is being sacrificed to globalism. As Mark Twain stated, "Loyalty to Country, ALWAYS! Loyalty to Government, when it deserves it."

Honor is the glue that could awaken and unite many. A club/group did form with many of my classmates, called "Men of Meat," posited in patriotic, "carnivore" good fun. The group is led by a very personable classmate, who not surprisingly works for the International Monetary Fund. As a result, will they serve as "armchair warriors," motivated by politically correct, albeit inaccurate, perspectives (Israel is our best friend, we need to kill "ragheads," etc.), or might they, through conscientious fellowship, evolve into the much needed Veterans League of Honor? I hope to join, and trust that I will not be seen as a renegade, a "Jiminy Cricket" to be avoided or condemned.

"The further a society drifts from the truth, the more it will hate those that speak it." —GEORGE ORWELL

Of other concern is how our Academies, as premiere training grounds for our officer corps, are potential targets for subversion. For example, two brothers of Israeli origin went to West Point with backgrounds suggesting they were American. How this happened should be addressed. After serving short tours, they formed security companies, which gained contracts with the NSA and Department of Defense. In complex manner, they and Mossad-spawned companies infiltrated our highest levels of government, essentially handing the keys to our most sensitive computers and communications systems to Israel.[1]

At a West Point class reunion, a friend and general officer commented that he had to return to his post early, as he had an Israeli delegation to give a VIP tour to. This concerns me in light of the fact that there is an imbalance in the exchange of information and, in fact, there should be no exchange of information with Israel. Former Mossad officer Victor Ostrovsky, in his book *By Way of Deception*, reveals how the Mossad has worked to undermine American security interests and often endears and imbeds itself with the American military and government agencies to gain classified information and to leverage for Israeli interests. He cites examples, which indicate that this is never reciprocated in a balanced way by their military or intelligence services. More recently it has been revealed that Israel has stolen U.S. technological secrets and sold them to China.

At the same reunion, a Jewish classmate who I had considered one of my best West Point friends (he was in our wedding) became very distant when I mentioned the USS *Liberty* story. Subsequently, I would get group emails from him denigrating any and all enemies of Israel and calling for actions against the Iranians. When I challenged that discourse and reminded him that Israel had attacked the USS *Liberty*, and Iran was being unfairly condemned, he cut off email communications with the parting shot that Israel was America's best friend and he would hear no criticism of them. In my mind, I could only question why his loyalty was not simply to America, to military veterans (including the crew of the USS *Liberty*), and to the unrestrained pursuit of truths.

Currently, our military services are comprised of a very small percent of Jewish men and women—1/3 of 1%, as compared to their 2-3% representation within America's general population. However, a surprising number volunteer to serve in the Israeli Defense Forces.

Despite the low representation at our troop level, U.S. senior command positions are disproportionately staffed by officers with a discomforting level of support for the Zionist agenda, especially during the period just before and since 9/11.[2]

Of additional concern for our military is the prospect that abuses have been committed at places like Guantanamo Bay, Abu Ghraib and elsewhere. Soldiers, under stress and without positive leadership, can resort to brutal behavior. America has always prided itself on striving for better. It is most distressful that Congress passed and the president signed into law "The Military Commissions Act of 2006," for it violates the principle of habeas corpus, encouraging further abuses, similar to Israel's treatment of Palestinian detainees. Likewise, Patriot Act/Freedom Act provisions victimize innocent people and deny them due process and protections normally afforded under the law. These are serious transgressions by our political leaders. We must demand better of our lawmakers and hold the judiciary accountable in fulfilling their responsibilities, in accordance with our Constitution, to challenge these unfair laws. Increasingly, however, court rulings seem to defy logic, fairness and any reasonable constitutional interpretation. This is partially due to the nature of the political appointment process, and a lack of subsequent oversight, or term limits.

On a final note of grave consequence for our military is the experimentation and use of inhumane weapons. In both Iraq wars there was evidence that the U.S. used depleted uranium weapons. The direct consequence is excessive and latent cancers and bizarre birth abnormalities occurring to Iraqis and to American servicemen and their families.[3] There is evidence that Israel used phosphorous bombs against the Lebanese as well as tens of thousands of cluster bomblets, which remained dispersed throughout the countryside and continue to kill innocent civilians. These weapons were introduced despite being in violation of the protocols of the Geneva Convention or other international bodies.[4] The long-term effects of these weapons is devastation to their populations and environs. Israel has also used an experimental weapon against Palestinian civilians, which is similar to a U.S. developed weapon called the DIME (Dense Inert Metal Explosive). These weapons cause amputations and severe burns and are also believed to be carcinogenic.[5] This is reprehensible and violates all sense of humanity. Unbelievably, use continued in the recent Gaza massacres, and was not condemned by America's leadership or media.

Thankfully, some service academy graduates are trying to reveal the truths about the deceptions that led us into Iraq and subverted our foreign policy to Israel's benefit and to select business interests. A few formed West Point Graduates Against the War (www.wpaw.org). There are also alternative news outlets that report military and political outrages, in opposition to the propaganda emanating from the controlled mainstream media. The most effective are http://VeteransToday.com, http://VeteransNewsNow.com, and http://VeteransTruthNetwork.com.

**CHAPTER NOTES:**

1 "Israelis Hold Keys to NSA and US Government Computers," *American Free Press*, Sept. 4, 2006.

2 "A Perfect Storm? Obama and the Zionist Power Configuration," Edmund Connelly, *Occidental Observer*, Nov 16, 2008.

3 A. William Lewis video, "Beyond Treason," Power Hour Productions, 2005.

4 Robert Fisk, "The Mystery of Israel's Secret Uranium Bomb," *The Washington Report on Middle East Affairs*, December 2006.

5 Meron Rapoport, "Italian Probe: Israel Used New Weapon Prototype in Gaza Strip," *Ha'aretz*, October 11, 2006.

FRÉDÉRIC BASTIAT

# CHAPTER 10

# Foreign Policy

"When goods do not cross borders, soldiers will."
—FRÉDÉRIC BASTIAT

꧁❃꧂

**H**UMILITY AND RESTRAINT: Decades of war decimated many Western nations during the 20th century, including Britain, France, Germany, and Russia. Each mistakenly believed that their imperialist policies and actions would yield greater benefits at home and abroad. America has no moral obligation, or right, to spread our culture, values or institutions to non-Western nations, particularly in the Middle East. A non-interventionist position is the only way to guide America's international policy.

However, so-called experts, through media promotion, convince us of the wisdom of supporting aggressive internationalist policies to "spread democracy" —in total defiance to the best interests and will of the American people. These well-promoted "elites" include such luminaries as Henry Kissinger and Zbigniew Brzezinski, who have founded and been leaders of several globalist institutions. When first entering the film industry, I read a book, *The Kid Stays in the*

Henry Kissinger

*Picture* by Robert Evans (nee Shapera), who as head of Paramount Pictures gloated over their success in constructing a public image for Henry Kissinger. They utilized his guttural speech impairment to promote a persona of genius. A friend interviewed Kissinger much later for a book and remarked how unremarkable he seemed to be, yet concerned for his legacy. This was many years ago, yet they still roll Kissinger and Brzezinski out for international strategic "redirects."

As a sovereign nation, we must refuse to be strong-armed by the international community to serve the interests of others. The lives of our youth must not be sacrificed for international disputes that have no bearing on the welfare of the American people. The United States should re-evaluate its relationships with the United Nations and NATO and close most of the Pentagon's hundreds of overseas military bases. At the same time, a strong military for legitimate defense must be maintained, such as better protection of U.S. borders.

## STATE DEPARTMENT

U.S. foreign policy has been a continuous series of mistakes, misjudgments, failures and political errors. We have had a sequence of CFR (Council on Foreign Relations), TC (Trilateral Commission), and Bilderberger Secretaries of State whose fundamental understanding of economy and foreign policy is seriously flawed.

American foreign policy is largely developed by "study groups" within the CFR—mostly academics and proponents for the military-industrial complex, multinational corporations, and even foreign powers. Israel exercises a hugely disproportionate influence on U.S. foreign policy through AIPAC, the CFR, several neocon think tanks, and the mainstream media. Current policies, especially on Middle East issues, are not based on American interests, but on Israeli hegemony in the region. Many dual-citizens staff the Middle East desks at State and that does not produce an evenhanded foreign policy.

As George Washington said, "A passionate attachment of one nation for another produces a variety of evils." Throughout most of our early history, America was viewed as isolationist—due to our geographic position, but also due to our nature of "minding our own business." America is a country which has prospered and led by example. It is most proud of its constitutional heritage. The republican form of government has served us well and our independent attitude has usually been tempered with generous humanitarian actions. As Thomas Jefferson said, "The care of human life and happiness, and not their destruction, is the first and only object of good government."

Over the last hundred years however, we have increasingly become more international and aggressive. Our incursions into the Middle East have been regarded by the rest of the world as imperialistic. We now take "pre-emptive" actions against perceived threats. More and more, these are revealed to be deceits, which are leading us down a totalitarian path of virulent aggression. Our "Shock and Awe" campaign against Iraq was an illegal and unjust act based on lies. It was spearheaded by "neocon planners," one of whom, Paul Wolfowitz, instead of being vilified was promoted to president of the World Bank.

John Quincy Adams once said, *"America does not go abroad in search of monsters to destroy. She is the well-wisher to the freedom and independence of all. She is the champion and vindicator only of her own."* By nature, Americans were not military "empire builders," but in recent years, we have become the weapon's arm of an intended "Israeli empire." Going back to 1942, Zionists' plans included eventually transferring the Arab population of Palestine to Iraq[1] and gaining regional hegemony. It seems as if our destructive efforts, throughout the Middle East, are in partial fulfillment of Zionist plans.

In 2006, two academics, John J. Mearsheimer and Stephen M. Walt, published a paper entitled "The Israel Lobby and U.S. Foreign Policy." First published in a British journal, it would gain momentum through the Internet and begin to receive some "under the radar" attention in the U.S. The paper is a study of the excessive influence that the Israeli lobby, and in particular The American-Israel Public Affairs Committee (AIPAC), has on American foreign policy decisions. They postulate that the Lobby has an unacceptable degree of control over our foreign policy decisions, which is not in the best interests of America. In 1985, this was the principle theme of former Illinois Congressman Paul Findley's *They Dare to Speak Out.* This should not be news to anyone who has studied the international scene over the last 40 years, but it seems to create a great deal of consternation in any public forum, quite possibly because of the troubling degree of influence that the lobby's chief agents in our government and private sector have come to exercise. Any resistance to their Israel-first agenda will create a special interest backlash, which for any politician will lead to a highly-funded ouster.

Neocon agents for Israel-first have enmeshed us in the Middle East to the benefit of Israel and certain business interests, but certainly not to the benefit of the American people or the indigenous populations. As a nation, our primary response since 9/11 has been to wage war against "Arab radicals," despite the fact that any linkage to Iraq was contrived. The Muslim people are generally compassionate and fair-minded; however, extreme elements will appear and with violent retort when unjust persecutions are allowed to go unfettered. CIA analyst Michael Scheuer, who wrote *Imperial Hubris* anonymously, makes the great case that all our difficulties with the Arab world relate to our unquestioning support for Israel and that the root evil is Israel's continued occupation of Palestinian lands and subjugation of the indigenous peoples.[2] Until this injustice is addressed by America, which otherwise continues to blindly bankroll the Israeli war machine, we will continue to be at odds with the Islamic world.

## THE UNITED NATIONS

The United States of America should reevaluate its relationship with the United Nations and its ancillary organizations. As a consequence of leveraged actions on behalf of global elitists, the United Nations increasingly imposes its will on sovereign nations, to the detriment of our own national interests. The globalist "Agenda 21" and other international plans, which are decreed on member nations, are not only costly and oppressive, but demand a forfeiture of national sovereignty, and, for us, subordination of constitutional U.S. laws and our guaranteed rights and freedoms. This is not what our forefathers fought for.

The UN spends billions of dollars on efforts that seldom bring any benefit to the United States or other independent nations. It was supposed to end wars, but has been totally ineffective, as more wars have been fought since its establishment, in 1945, than at any previous time in mankind's history.

## FOREIGN AID

We must reject the idea that the U.S. forever subsidize Third World countries. Charity must begin and end at home and be the domain of individuals and philanthropic organizations, not government. Foreign aid, except approved forms of emergency relief and relocation efforts, should be terminated. Today, when the United States has not a single strong adversary (except for terrorist organizations that we create), foreign aid has become an unnecessary and wasteful expenditure. The vast majority of foreign aid (90%) winds up in the hands of ruling juntas, and the people of those countries gain nothing. As Ron Paul succinctly pointed out, *"Foreign aid is poor people of a wealthy country giving to wealthy people of a poor country."*

The largest portion of American foreign aid goes to Israel, whose national per capita income is between that of Italy and Spain, neither of which get foreign aid. So long as the U.S. continues giving Israel $3 billion foreign aid, and $5 billion military aid (and also billions of dollars in "loans" that are never repaid) Israel will continue to create havoc for America and resentment from its enemies. Current presidential candidates (including all of the frontrunners) are clamoring for more aid to Israel…who do they work for?

America's government has been corrupted away from the vision of its Founders and now surreptitiously serves international financial interests. As a result, America is currently being sacrificed as a "warrior empire" to serve the global elites, rather than its own people. We have apathetically abandoned our responsibility to hold government agents accountable. As a republic, these representatives should be bound by strict constitutional limits and not allowed to self-servingly grow government to monstrous proportions.

If the American republic can be honestly restored to once again lead by positive example (rather than imperial force), then we have a chance to defeat these international forces of tyranny. The great battle requires nations to respect sovereignty and seek truth and justice, such that freedom and peace can prevail.

CHAPTER NOTES:

1 *The Zionist Connection II*, Alfred M. Lilienthal, p. 32.

2 *Imperial Hubris*, Anonymous [later revealed to be by Michael Scheuer], Brassey's, 2004, p, 200.

GEN. WESLEY CLARK

# CHAPTER 11

# *Iran*

"We're going to take out seven countries in five years, starting with Iraq, and then Syria, Lebanon, Libya, Somalia, Sudan, and finishing off, Iran."
—GENERAL WESLEY CLARK, relating content of a post-9/11 Secretary of Defense memo

IRAN IS CLEARLY THE MOST FORMIDABLE OF ISRAEL'S ENEMIES in the Middle East and globalists are working feverishly to justify a war to remove this obstacle to their end game. In recent years, all roads of aggression in the Middle East, including Afghanistan, Iraq, Libya, and Syria, have been meant to circumscribe Iran. As a leader in the Islamic world and a vibrant nation, Iran has resisted foreign encroachments and tyranny against innocent peoples of the world, including the Palestinians.

Azadi Square, Tehran

Despite the ongoing and fanatical rhetoric, Iran has been no threat to the United States and hasn't attacked another country in hundreds of years. Israel, on the other hand, has started or been engaged in multiple wars since its founding in 1948, and now advocates for war against Iran. This kind of posturing got America involved in the unjust war against Iraq—another of Israel's enemies. The current saber rattling is supported by the American "mainstream" media and is largely based on Israeli intelligence manipulations. (The Mossad's motto is "By way of deception, thou shalt do war")

The battles are not just against Iran, but any and all nation-states (currently Syria) that seek to protect their people and their national sovereignty from this international tyranny. The internationalists derive their greatest power from control of centralized banking. Target nations have resisted globalist takeovers of their economies, which is why Iran was singled out as part of an "axis of evil" and has been subject to unfair scrutiny and sanctions.

Over three years ago, I made my first of several trips to Iran and reported on my findings. An article was published in international journals and periodicals, and by several alternative media sources in America, but not by any U.S. mainstream media outlets. My submission of this report, and an accompanying PressTV interview (YouTube: "US Presidential Candidate says, 'Israel did 911' Zionists Control US Politics") were posted at "First Call," an on-line magazine for West Point graduates. The report and video were removed within two days by neocon screeners who unfortunately censor critical and truthful news that might be damaging to Israeli or neocon interests, even when the facts are critical to America's best interests.

As then reported:

> I contemplate my September 2012 trip to the Islamic Republic of Iran and ask myself who wants war between America and Iran. I quickly surmise that it is not the American people, nor the Iranian people, but globalists (international bankers and their multinational beneficiaries). They control Israel, the American media and most of our politicians . . . and by extension our foreign policy.
>
> My journey to this exotic and little understood land began with an invitation to "New Horizon—The First Inter-

national Independent Filmmakers Festival." It was a conference and festival held in Tehran. Filmmakers and intellectuals from around the world attended. It was one of the most stimulating experiences that I have ever had and an effective bridge between diverse cultures and perspectives—with the purpose of promoting truth, justice, liberty, and peace.

This initiative was undertaken, not by America or other world leaders, but by a country unfairly besieged with sanctions and threats of war. My observations were in stark contrast to the perceptions of most Americans. What I experienced was a devout country with a love of God, family, and nation—and an uncompromising respect for the noblest of human endeavors.

As I write this, a giant, beautiful book, *Rubaiyat of Omar Khayyam*, lies next to me. Khayyam's wonderful poems have survived the test of time and are a testament to the normally peaceful spirit of the Persian people. This treasure was given to me by President Mahmoud Ahmadinejad. Inside its back cover, he inscribed the following for me (transcribed from Farsi):

In the name of God who loves human beings.

My dear brother:

I, you, we and all of us are pursuing truth and happiness for human beings, which is unfortunately a victim of world powers.

This is a historical opportunity to undermine all inhuman relations and put an end to prejudices, which have questioned the truths and separates them, to build a new beautiful world based on love, justice and beauty.

This is a historical and certainly achievable objective. It only needs our hands, minds and hearts to join each other.

I pray Great God to bless you, who love humanity and wish success for all. I hope to meet you in a better future.

(signed)
M. Ahmadinejad
September 8, 2012

Shaking President Ahmadinejad's hand.

I found President Ahmadinejad to be a humble man with a firm handshake and intense, intelligent eyes. Despite his courteous and dignified bearing, he has been regularly berated, and routinely misrepresented by a controlled western media [his purported threat "We will wipe Israel off the map" was an intentional misquote]. Is demonization justified, or has he been targeted as the lone political figure standing against Zionist powers? This is my attempt to represent truths, such that the world might have a better understanding of Iran, its people, and its leadership.

The Iranian people are similar to Europeans in appearance . . . a beautiful people, poised and kind. Their women wear clothing which modestly cover them, but in elegant fashion and with serene faces that are usually exposed. They return smiles and are not treated as second-class citizens, as we have been conditioned to believe. In fact, they outnumber men in higher education enrollments. There is no profanity and women are safe on any Tehran street—at any time of day or night. The influences of Western civilization have not been totally removed, but the Iranians resist the decadence of Cultural Marxism. I attribute this largely to their faith and love of family.

I was surprised to discover that the Islamic faith actually honors Jesus and Christianity. However, through Zionist media control, policy dictates, and other manipulations, the Christian world is incessantly convinced that Muslims should be our enemies and that we should be theirs.

Iman Square, Isfahan

Muslims look with jaundiced eye upon the outrageous media lies and perpetual assaults on their faith and culture. Hollywood's promotion of twisted films can provoke extremist reactions, and we are then led to believe that Muslims are all radicals. We never question the bizarre promotion of these divisive, Zionist-inspired productions, or the actions of multinational interests in the internal affairs of sovereign Islamic nations. Were we to look honestly at the many false portrayals, we would see remarkable similarities to how our Christian communities have also been assaulted—increasingly with contempt and disrespect by these same Zionist and cultural Marxist propagandists. They seek a globalist new world order—devoid of the diversity and freedoms associated with independent nation-states.

As I wandered from the festival grounds to meet people on the streets, I found them to be most helpful and without animosity—despite my obvious American nationality. I enjoyed their exotic food and came to appreciate the craftsmanship of their products. The only negative sensation that I had was in witnessing the mad house traffic situation in Tehran. A city of 15 million, it has grown faster that it's infrastructure. Despite this, the city is thriving with new construction and beautiful parks and monuments—which reflect a noble and accomplished people. The Iranians seemingly love Americans, but are rightly concerned and critical of our irrational and invasive government policies. The common response seems to be "why would your country want to attack us?"

The current condemnation of Iran is supposedly due to the possibility that they may develop nuclear weapons. We should all work for a world free from nuclear threat, but the sovereignty of nations must also be respected. Iran is signatory to the Nuclear Non-Proliferation Treaty and has opened their facilities for inspection, declaring their interest is for energy development only. No evidence to the contrary has been shown, and Iran's Supreme Leader, the Ayatollah Khamenei condemns nuclear weaponry—actually declaring a "Fatwa" against them—as it is contrary to their nation's faith.

However, Israel, their chief accuser (and architect behind the campaign to falsely accuse Iraq of possessing "weapons of mass destruction"), is believed to possess over 300 nuclear weapons. Israel is not a signatory to the Nuclear Non-Proliferation Treaty and has no intention of sharing information or opening their facilities for inspection—yet America continues to march to their fanatical war drums against others.

Why is there no pressure on Israel to meet the same standards and why are we imposing "sanctions" against a nation that has done us no wrong? It is a preliminary act of war, and only imposed because Israeli lobbies demand it of our lap-dog politicians, who incredibly serve Zionist interests rather than the American people.

UN Secretary-General Ban Ki-moon and Iran's
supreme leader, Ayatollah Khamenei.

Iran is a strategic rival for regional hegemony in the resource rich Middle East and has stood strong for Islamic
unity. They also courageously and most justifiably call for
an end to the Palestinian occupation—the ruthless suppression of an enslaved people, largely funded by America.
There is no greater injustice than that being perpetrated
against the Palestinian people. World condemnation,
through the United Nations, is consistently blocked by U.S.
actions on the Security Council. As a result, the Non-
Aligned Movement (NAM) of nations is growing as an alternative to the UN. Its recent success is not generally
reported in Western media, but 120 nations came together
in Tehran the week before the New Horizon Film Festival—
in unity and in opposition to the evils of the Israeli occupation of Palestine. The secretary general of the United
Nations even attended, as well as observers from Russia and
China. The Palestinian occupation and Israeli aggressions
(including false-flag operations against other nations) are
at the root of the discontents for Zionism.

As President Ahmadinejad gave me a copy of Khayyam's
works, I gave him a copy of my western motion picture,
"Jericho," and my political book, *Our Vision for America*.
When I asked him what messages I might convey to the

American people, he indicated "truths" and "Iran's desire for peace." Through lies and evil acts, globalists and Zionists falsely portray Iran, as they seek conflict between nations. I later told him that our State Department should be meeting with Iran's leaders and not depending on the initiatives of private citizens, like me. However, I hope that he and the Iranian people take hope in the prospect that many patriotic Americans are awakening to the evils that have consumed us, even while our politicians continue to betray the otherwise good spirit and traditions of the American people. Growing numbers seek answers that might save America and truly promote world peace.

Americans do not want war, and are beginning to realize that our politicians, of both major parties, initiate these actions against the wishes of the American people—and in accord with the intrigues of international bankers and their Zionist agents. It is time we stopped them by creating alternatives in politics, and in media. Iran sees the need and is taking appropriate initiatives, and so should America.

Milad Tower, Tehran

I went to Iran to promote the prospects for producing "False Flag," a critically important motion picture. I returned to America more committed than ever to produce this political thriller and, through commercial entertainment, help awaken a sleeping America. Vital truths must be revealed so that new evils are not perpetrated against the people of America and Iran, with destructive effects resonating throughout the world. I also return committed to building a viable third party, which will represent traditional working-class Americans, rather than perpetuating a corrupt two-party system, which serves special global interests. God willing, my answer to the courageous efforts of President Ahmadinejad is "I also hope to meet you in a better future."

I would like to state that I am most proud of the many filmmakers, journalists, and intellectuals who visited Iran during those difficult days, and who I was fortunate to befriend. They are heroes in my mind and include such courageous international truth seekers as French comedian and satirist Dieudonne, political journalist Thierry Meyssan, legal journalist Dr. Franklin Lamb, "Truth Jihad Radio" host Dr. Kevin Barrett, author/analyst F. William Engdahl, *Culture Wars*'s Dr. E. Michael Jones, investigative author Dr. James Fetzer, former Marine and MV *Mavi Marmara* hero Ken O'Keefe, economist/author Rodney Shakespeare, World Trade Center hero William Rodriguez, developer/filmmaker Art Olivier, author/geostrategist Manuel Galiana, and many others.

Dr. E. Michael Jones and Dr. Kevin Barrett in Iran.

Since that first trip and my last one earlier this year, I am pleased by the diplomatic efforts to restore a more normal relationship between our countries. This will hopefully not be sabotaged by irrational Israeli/neocon forces, which unfortunately still dominate American politics. They are very concerned with any effort to improve relations between Iran and America.

One Saturday morning, just prior to my last trip, I needed a haircut and, with my wife accompanying me, entered my local barber shop. A moment later, a short, but fit, swarthy man entered. He was wearing a jacket with Hebrew letters, and an Israeli patch on the shoulder. This is a most unusual site for a small town in the Smoky Mountains. His hair was professionally coiffed, not a regular of east Tennessee. He sat strategically, with back to the wall and to the side and rear of the barber, covertly observing us. He was seemingly listening (with earbud) to his "smart" phone, while simultaneously texting. He had a belly pack which he would abruptly open and close, monitoring our reactions. I covertly gave message to my wife, as we read periodicals. There were three other customers in front of me. After about 45 minutes, my turn came. As I sat in the chair, I kept my hands hidden beneath the apron, while the "tourist" would repeatedly rise and sit in his chair... to the bewilderment of the barber. As I was about finished, the man suddenly left the shop, indicating that he'd be back on Monday. I'm sure that, instead, his next haircut was in NYC, or DC, or Tel Aviv. I suspect that his mission was to observe, intimidate, and gauge reactions. I didn't report this to my area FBI representatives. However, I do believe that many agents are now figuring things out and quietly working to reclaim our country. They were most interested in my unique Homeland Security experiences (see http://MerlinMiller.com/homeland-security-or-tyranny/).

For those who study the geopolitical situation from a strategic standpoint, I believe that the 1979 Iranian Revolution was a key event in history. The 1953 CIA organized coup overthrew the democratically elected President Mosaddegh and installed the Shah. Mosaddegh was restructuring the oil industry to benefit the Iranians, and not British and American corporate interests. By 1979, Iranian resentments, especially to the Shah's tyranny and discovery that the American Embassy was a den of Mid-East spying, eventually led to Iran's throwing off the yoke of foreign control.

My belief is that international central bankers, who had played the Cold War to its limits, thereafter decided to facilitate a Soviet collapse and subsequent co-opting of Russia (the oligarchs made their move under Yeltsin). The Middle East could then be restructured to benefit a struggling Israel, Western oil interests and the war machine. Ultimately, the "War on Terror" would be engineered to pit the Christian and Muslim worlds against each other—satisfying many ambitions, to include establishing a tyrannical New World Order. However, Russian President Vladimir Putin has surprised, and frustrated, the puppet masters—challenging their centuries-old, ruthless dominance.

ALEKSANDR SOLZHENITSYN

# *Russia*

"You must understand, the leading Bolsheviks who took over Russia were not Russians. They hated Russians. They hated Christians. Driven by ethnic hatred they tortured and slaughtered millions of Russians without a shred of human remorse. It cannot be overstated. Bolshevism committed the greatest human slaughter of all time. The fact that most of the world is ignorant and uncaring about this enormous crime is proof that the global media is in the hands of the perpetrators."

—ALEKSANDR SOLZHENITSYN

**N**O COUNTRY HAS BEEN more traumatized during the last 100 years than Russia. The Bolshevik Revolution, the World Wars, the ruthless purges and the satanic effects of communism were to nearly destroy the lifeblood of the nation. The surviving people were denied their basic freedoms and lived in fear and dependence of a tyrannical centralized government. With that in mind,  and having experienced another life-changing trip, my wife and I submitted the following report for publication consideration. No mainstream sources showed any interest, but it has been published by many alternative media outlets.

# Russia . . . War or Peace?

### By Merlin Miller

On May 30, 2015, my wife, Susan, and I joined a small delegation of concerned citizens to visit Russia, a nation under Western media and political assault, and economic sanctions.

Organized by Sharon Tennison, founder of the Center for Citizen Initiatives (http://ccisf.org/), this independent, one-of-a-kind sojourn was to extend "grassroots goodwill" by meeting directly with the Russian people. Our goal was to learn truths and perspectives first-hand, rather than rely on a special-interests controlled mass media, which in- creasingly and unfairly demonizes the "land of white nights" and their leader, President Vladimir Putin.

CCI travelers first went to Russia (the former Soviet Union) in 1983 to help usher in a climate of positive exchanges. The organization ultimately sponsored

Sharon Tennison
Founder of CCI

over 6,000 Russian entrepreneurs to visit and train in America, while leading American expeditions to Russia. Although largely unheralded, these efforts helped create a political thaw (Glasnost and Perestroika), which helped to normalize relations between the two powers. Unfortunately, citizens' initiatives are once again needed to help restore positive relations between America and Russia, and to challenge the misguided foreign policies that threaten world peace.

Our group visited four regions over 17 days; Moscow, Volgograd, Ekaterinburg, and St. Petersburg. While we did meet some government officials and media representatives, our focus was people-to-people, interacting with the growing number of Russian entrepreneurs who are creating a new middle class and a strong future for their country.

In Moscow, we were greeted with an impressive mix of grand architecture and modern facilities. The city, now numbering nearly 14 million people, was vibrant. Their subway system was impeccable, with a palace-like decor, including crystal chandeliers . . . and their trains ran on time!

Underground in the Moscow metro.

The Russian people were physically fit and better dressed than contemporary Americans. We found no hostility among them and they were uniformly helpful. As Americans, we were probably perceived as loud and obnoxious, while they were quiet and cautiously respectful. Much of their demeanor, as we were to learn, has developed over centuries of subordination to authorities in addition to living in such close quarters to each other. Individual noise levels had to be subdued in public and in thin-walled apartments throughout the Soviet years. The era of the czars and nearly a century of communism seem to have taken an irrefutable toll on their individualism, but we sensed a growing entrepreneurial spirit, optimism and sense of national pride.

It appeared to me that our nations are going through bizarre role reversals. They have expectations of greater freedom and prosperity, while we are experiencing a loss of liberty and wealth, and a sense of uncertain desperation. To date, they reject "Western Cultural Marxism," which has been destroying American society. Ironically, this cultural Marxist assault on America's traditional institutions had its birth in communist (and socialist) doctrines, which the Russians increasingly reject.

While in Moscow we also met with a large group of students at The Moscow School of Social and Economic Sciences, who seek future exchanges. They were eager to learn American ways, at least those which they perceived as healthy and productive. The freedoms and pioneering spirit, which had been foreign to the Russian people before the successes of groups like CCI and Rotary International, are becoming increasingly real. I was reminded of the optimism of growing up in Iowa in the 1950s and '60s, before the subversion of our inspired traditions.

Saint Basil Cathedral in Red Square.

After a few days in Moscow, we took the overnight train south to Volgograd (known as Stalingrad during WWII). We met several Russian soldiers on the train who were part of a military band and eager to practice their English. What fun they were and how helpful in negotiating for snacks from the "babushkas" at the occasional stops. Upon arrival in Volgograd, we were greeted by a score of local entrepreneurs, extending flowers to our women and helping with baggage. Many of them had participated in CCI and Rotary programs and warmly greeted our special petite Sharon, who had so positively impacted their lives. Over the next few days we were invited to private "dashas" for dinner, to Rotary meetings, clinics, and entrepreneurial ventures. It was inspiring to witness these individual business enterprises, a few of which had grown to be enormously successful.

While in the river port city, we gained a deep appreciation for the sacrifices of the Russian people. The Battle of Stalingrad (Volgograd) had been the turning point in WWII. The Germans were committed to taking the strategic river port city and the Russians had to first defend for survival, before counterattacking and ultimately prevailing.

A remnant from "The Battle of Stalingrad"/Volgograd.

Although the city was decimated and nearly 3 million people lost their lives (approximately 2 million Russian men, women and children, and 1 million German soldiers), the people have stoically rebuilt. They know the horrors of war, and honor their fallen with incredible monuments. More than we can possibly appreciate, they have suffered and sincerely seek a future of peace.

The Motherland monument, situated on the high ground of Volgograd.

We next flew to Ekaterinburg, just east of the Ural Mountains and technically in Siberia (Asia). This industrial city had been a primary producer of war materials during the Second World War, as it was more distant from the battlefields. It is the city where Czar Nicholas II and his family had been sequestered, and then brutally executed by the Bolsheviks in 1918. Today, the Ekaterinburg region suffers from aging factories but is seeking new investment and production possibilities, and is most interested in improved relations with America. Our group did visit the American Consulate, where the consul general's political perspectives seemed to be at odds with the realities that we experienced, and some of our members expressed dissatisfaction with his representations.

The Church on the Blood, where Czar Nicholas II and his family were executed.

My wife and I were hosted for a side trip to Chelybinsk, where we viewed some real estate projects and met community leaders who were eager for development support. As an outlying area, federal supports are less visible than in the major centers, and this seemed to be of some concern, especially at this time of economic sanctions.

On the Silk Road, between East and West, in Chelybinsk.

The last and most impressionable leg of our visit was to Saint Petersburg (known as Leningrad during WWII). Built by Peter the Great, the city is regarded as "the Venice of the North" with beautiful canals and magnificent buildings, palaces and churches.

Saint Petersburg was surrounded by German forces from September 1941 until January 1944 ("the Siege of Leningrad"). Although much was destroyed and the people suffered greatly, the city miraculously survived, and restoration efforts have restored its magnificence. Several outlying palaces, including the Peterhof, Pavlosk, and Tsarskoye Selo, were under the control of the Germans. We toured the famous Amber Room, which had been pillaged of its panels but since wonderfully recreated.

The city of Saint Petersburg is now a magnet for cruise lines and has become an international destination, uniquely blending European and Russian cultures. Renowned for its Baroque architecture, museums, mosaics, ballets and symphonies, the city is a wondrous experience. We saw no obvious poverty and, since the Putin era, renovations have accelerated. Corruption has been significantly reduced, and there is also a growing sense of fiscal responsibility. During the recent celebration of their WWII victory, which unfortunately was snubbed by America—the city spent more funds than anticipated. As a result, they cancelled the fireworks display that had been scheduled for the subsequent celebration of The Day of Russia (commemorating the anniversary of the birth of the new Russia, after communism). We cruised the River Neva during this celebration, enjoying the natural and manmade beauty, and respecting their decision. We wondered if politicians in America would show such fiscal responsibility.

Saint Petersburg's—Cathedral of the Resurrection.

Since the fall of the Soviet Empire, the Russian Orthodox Church is being resurrected and the people are finding a renewed spirituality, in contrast to the loss of America's once dominant Christian faith.

With the Soviet collapse, the Warsaw Pact disbanded and Russia became a federation of republics. NATO should have likewise disbanded, but instead has expanded eastward, in violation of international agreements and threatening regional security and Russian sovereignty. If the truths were known about the Ukrainian situation, we would never have involved ourselves (similar to Iraq, Afghanistan, Libya, and Syria). However, to the benefit of international plotters [including State Department's Victoria Nuland, wife of PNAC co-founder Robert Kagan], a violent coup was orchestrated and civil war instigated—not surprisingly, adjacent to Russia's borders and in the control path of vital natural resources.

Through the International Monetary Fund, the Ukrainians are now deeply impoverished. We met several Ukrainians while in Russia, and they passionately urged restraint, so that the Ukrainian people can pursue self-determination, rather than continued victimization through foreign interference. "American Exceptionalism" is much resented and is certainly not in keeping with our traditions. Current politicians, in service to international special interests (rather than the American people), seem to have forgotten Thomas Jefferson's wise counsel . . . "peace, commerce, and honest friendship with all nations, entangling alliances with none." Other nations have their own "Monroe Doctrines" protective of their sovereign interests, which we should respect.

Noted journalist Robert Parry is perhaps the best analyst of the current situation. His articles lays bare the facts and reveal the propaganda and manipulations which have escalated these unnecessary and destructive conflicts. His latest example can be found at www.consortiumnews.com.

For comprehensive information, I highly recommend "Russia Insider" (http://russia-insider.com/en). We must reach beyond America's controlled mass media to find truths—once again born of journalistic integrity and personal ethics. Before being privileged to join Sharon Tennison's eclectic and stellar group, I had previously travelled to Iran (www.veteransnewsnow.com/2012/09/21/215335-as-the-israeli-war-drums-beat/), where I came to deeply respect the Iranian people and their often-misrepresented perspectives. In my quest for truths, I found that we must, as private citizens, seek our own answers and not depend on the perspectives of others.

Throughout our incredible trip, we gauged Russians' knowledge and attitudes of current events. They are much more politically aware than most Americans, probably because of the traumas that they have experienced during the last century, and sensing the current dangers. My wife and I came to have great respect for the Russian people and for our special delegation—which has returned, inspired to share truths in the cause of peace and humanity. The Russian people are very much like the American people, and we should pursue friendly relations. I encourage everyone to support the work of the Center for Citizen Initiatives (http://ccisf.org/).

In closing, I'd like to share my wife's perspectives. During our first night back home, and after having experienced 17 days of stimulation and very little sleep, she awoke inspired to write her reflections.

# Reflections from Russia

### By Susan Miller

A s I reflect on my journey to Russia, I am transported once again to the elaborate hall of mirrors in Catherine's Palace. I see different images in each of the many reflections that surround me.

The mirror closest to me shows the love that people have for each other, for family, country, and humanity. This was reflected every day in a gesture, a loving smile, hug, kiss, or a sincere handshake. I see the same gestures of love among people in America. Are we so different from each other?

Across the room I see reflected the image of respect. First and foremost a subtle self-respect. It is shown in the posture of the men, women, youth, and even the children. They hold themselves erect, head high, and they even look you in the eye when they talk to you. I am not sure that I see that anymore in America. Are we losing our self-respect?

Another image that I see is sorrow. An image reflected at the WWII monuments which dominate the landscape of Volgograd and the entrance to Saint Petersburg. The sorrow is reflected in the magnificence of the statue of the Motherland, the statues of soldiers helping wounded soldiers, of people helping people, and of a mother holding her dead son. The eternal flame, the lists of names, 900 lights for 900 days of the Saint Petersburg siege, and a magnificent diorama contribute to this overwhelming sorrow. These are not victory sites, but monuments depicting the sorrows of war, and crimes against humanity. We have such sites in America too. Gettysburg and Arlington come to mind as places that reflect the overwhelming sorrow of war. Does this Russia, that builds such monuments to the tragedy of war, truly want another war?

In each of the many mirrors I see reflected the people that I met. They do not smile easily, but when they do it is genuine and reflected in their eyes. The people are very reserved, especially in public and among strangers. You do not see them talking loud, laughing, arms moving or feet tapping. This is very different from the vivacious and noisy people of America. But does this make the Russians cold, or simply reflect a people who have been taught the need to guard their emotions?

Everywhere in the vast hall of mirrors I see reflected a country that has energy, and that is rising above its past history to become a land of new hope and opportunity. Most important, Russia is a place where people are finding their roots—in family, faith, values, and communities. We have so many things in common with the people of Russia, but I'm not sure if America's image to the world still reflects our values, our love of family, faith, and even freedom. Do we have roots in America anymore? Are we a country to be emulated? These are questions that I ask myself—as I reflect on the images in the mirror.

—SUSAN MILLER

Interestingly, Russia and China have sat on the sidelines, waiting and watching, as America self-destructs trying to build an empire at the behest of the Zionists. America's role may be short-lived, however, and then the Zionists may transfer their interests to another global power, if the time of their rule has not yet come. They did this in history with England, Russia, and Germany. China or the Pacific Rim may be their next target. As a side note, during Boris Yeltsin's corrupt regime in the mid-1990s, certain forces made a play to gain financial control of Russia. With Israeli and other international Jewish support, select thugs (who grew into Russian oligarchs) pilfered a desperate state of its resources in the name of newfound capitalism and supposed development. A brave Russian journalist, Paul Klebnikov, brought this thievery to international attention and was murdered for it. Subsequent cleanup actions by President Vladimir Putin have put the oligarchs on the run. Acting as a rational leader of his sovereign nation, President Putin has defied globalist ambitions. As a result, he has been unfairly represented and targeted—most effectively through coordinated disinformation campaigns about the Ukrainian and Syrian situations.

MARCUS TULLIUS CICERO

# CHAPTER 13

# *Money Matters*

"The Budget should be balanced, the Treasury should be refilled, public debt should be reduced, the arrogance of officialdom should be tempered and controlled, and the assistance to foreign lands should be curtailed, lest Rome will become bankrupt. People must again learn to work instead of living on public assistance." —CICERO, 55 B.C.

OR TOO LONG, THE AMERICAN REPUBLIC has been undermined by politicians who knowingly deceive the people and disregard their will. As Alexis de Tocqueville forecast, *"The American republic will endure until the day Congress discovers that it can bribe the public with the public's money."* The Republicans and Democrats have systematically collaborated in an effort to impose unwanted change on the nation. These "Republicrats" have leveraged against the people by limiting political choice, in disregard to the counsel of our forefathers.

## REPUBLIC UNDER ASSAULT

Throughout U.S. history, the vision of the Founding Fathers has been under continuous assault by international bankers, who have sought absolute control over people's lives and dominion throughout the world. The establishment of central banks was key to their plans.

One of the greatest scams imaginable, the Federal Reserve came into existence in 1913. It is neither federal, nor does it have reserves. Early in our history, central bankers tried to gain control of our country's economic system... twice they were defeated, first by Thomas Jefferson and later by Andrew Jackson. Several assassination attempts were made on the life of President Jackson and he related on his deathbed that his greatest success was, "I killed the bank."

Subsequent to Jackson's successes, the bankers would reorganize and plot well—advancing their global interests in numerous ways (Freemasonry, the communist movement, the Zionist movement, etc.). Approximately every 50 years they would orchestrate a new front.

Banker nemesis, President Andrew Jackson,
ironically pictured on the Fed's fiat currency.

They leveraged against America during the "Civil War" by surreptitiously pitting the states against each another. President Lincoln subsequently denied the states their constitutional right of secession, and began issuing executive orders, exceeding his authority. However, when he commissioned the issuance of Treasury "Greenbacks," instead of accepting loans at outrageous interest, he crossed the line with the international bankers. Lincoln's rejection of the Rothschild bank loan terms (at exorbitant interest) and issuance of his own Greenbacks, instead, set back their plans, but led to his eventual assassination. John Remington Graham's classic work, *Blood Money, the Civil War and the Federal Reserve*, lays out the manipulations leading to this unnecessary bloodbath and banker takeover of America.

The original 13th Amendment, which had disallowed those with titles of nobility or honor from holding office (essentially keeping lawyers from undermining the Constitution), was simply "replaced" with a new 13th Amendment—abolishing slavery. The Civil War was not fought over the morality of slavery but of economic hegemony. The deception, enabled by a selective promotion of history, has helped to preserve the hidden agenda of the moneyed interests.

After the Civil War, the 14th Amendment was invoked (but arguably never properly ratified), which began a process of enslaving the people to the federal government. The South's resistance led to the Reconstruction Act of 1867 and other infringements. President Andrew Johnson barely survived impeachment for his patriotic stand against the corrupt Congress. The Congress was not properly reconvened after the Civil War and it can be argued that a *de facto* government came into existence. The subsequent incorporation of The United States (District of Columbia and the Territories) began a series of incremental underminings of the Constitution and the subordination of our people—replacing common law with corporate law—whereby the people would become contractual subjects of the government.

With the next 50-year phase (1910s), the bankers finally achieved success through their control of President Woodrow Wilson and the enactment of the 16th and 17th Amendments and creation of their "Federal Reserve." President Wilson later expressed his regrets: "I am a most unhappy man. I have unwittingly ruined my country. A great industrial nation is controlled by its system of credit. Our system of credit is concentrated. The growth of the nation, therefore, and all our activities are in the hands of a few men. We have come to be one of the worst ruled, one of the most completely controlled and dominated Governments in the civilized world no longer a Government by free opinion, no longer a Government by conviction and the vote of the majority, but a Government by the opinion and duress of a small group of dominant men." Our financial serfdom, funded by the American taxpayer and aided by genocidal wars, would evolve over the next 100 years—leading to our now impending economic collapse.

Fifty years later, in the 1960s, a cultural revolution would be ushered in—to destroy the Christian religion and America's heritage, traditions, values, and the family unit—by pitting groups and individuals against each other. This insidious process has led to the country's current deplorable state and a final 50-year cycle—which the bankers believe will lead to our complete enslavement and submission to their planned one-world system.

## THE FEDERAL RESERVE

This privately owned consortium of international bankers work without constitutional authority and without any proper oversight to set monetary policy and issue a fiat currency. They unconscionably bilk the American taxpayers with never-ending interest charges on this currency—payment of which is assured through the creation of the IRS (also in 1913), which previously never existed and was not necessary for America's growth and prosperity. Despite people's misconceptions, the IRS could disappear today if we trimmed back federal expenditures to the level of our 2000 budget. Instead, the Fed and Treasury are now debt-financing multi-trillion dollar "bailouts" to Wall Street and private institutions, further indebting the American people and leading toward inevitable default. Where is the congressional responsibility and oversight?

Historically, protective tariffs and excise taxes were able to fund our federal expenditures. Deceptively, the IRS was actually created to be an enabler for the Federal Reserve System (interest payments to the bankers), an income redistributor (socialism), and a silent enslaver of the American people.

Our own Treasury should issue the currency, interest free, and it should be backed by silver or gold, as authorized by our Constitution. There are arguments for social credit alternatives to commodity backing, and careful analysis should be made to enable the most viable and honest solution—that does not involve colossal pilfering by private bankers. Distressingly, there is now increasing speculation that under President Lyndon Johnson, a large portion of the U.S. gold reserves, previously held at Ft. Knox, was surreptitiously removed and shipped out of country in 1968. The subsequent selling (at low fixed price) of remaining gold assets to foreign holders of U.S. debt is undoubtedly what precipitated the abandonment of our commodity backed currency by President Nixon in 1971. When will our public servants fulfill their responsibilities to the American people and demand an audit?

The only connection to real worth is now limited to our trust in a growing and increasingly oppressive government, controlled by these central bankers. By printing and injecting this new paper (a form of counterfeiting), all of our currency is devalued. The dollar today is worth approximately two cents compared to 1913 (when these shenanigans began). The real purchasing power of gold or silver has not changed substantially, which reveals how stable our currency could be and how much more affluent our people and country would be without the hidden tax of inflation.

The Federal Reserve also sets preferred government interest rates among banks, supposedly to help economic stability and to keep things in line with market conditions, but actually causing our economic "bubbles" and "bursts," undermining the true free market. Thomas Jefferson warned:

> I believe that banking institutions are more dangerous to our liberties than standing armies... If the American people ever allow private banks to control the issue of their currency, first by inflation, then by deflation, the banks and corporations that will grow up around [them] will deprive the people of all property until their children wake-up homeless on the continent their fathers conquered. The issuing power should be taken from the banks and restored to the people, to whom it properly belongs.

As the central banking system in America, the Fed also collaborates with the Bank of London, the Bank of International Settlements, the European Central Bank, the IMF, the World Bank and others (all part of the nefarious Rothschild network). They coordinate banking activities throughout the world, except for resistant "Axis of Evil" nations, which is why the politicians and media continue to selectively beat war drums against those "holdouts." The current hostility toward Russia is, in part, a result of their challenges to the global monetary system through their BRICS currency/trade bloc (Brazil, Russia, India, China, and South Africa). Currency wars are pending.

Throughout history, fiat currencies have led to the demise of empires. As our dollar becomes worth less, people on fixed incomes and lower wage earners are penalized and their wealth and security is essentially stolen. Also, as we gradually increase wage levels (always behind the curve), tax rates are higher, even though actual value is less. With our ongoing overseas military adventures, we are borrowing from countries like China, Japan and Saudi Arabia... billions of dollars per day! Politicians are passing on this debt to our kids, as they know that openly increasing taxes to pay for this would not be acceptable and they would be kicked out of office.

The ruling elite have accelerated a globalization agenda which favors the growth of government and multinational corporations. The crushing burden of taxation has been directed against the working middle class, while bailout monies enable huge bonuses to the

MONEY MATTERS | 123

cronies of those responsible for this banking mismanagement and appropriation of wealth. To get professional insights and more specifics on these financial shenanigans, one can look at the many writings and speeches of former Congressman Ron Paul (see www.campaignforliberty.com). Dr. Paul dressed down former Federal Reserve Chairmen Alan Greenspan and Ben Bernanke, and they always conceded—yet Dr. Paul was not able to get others in Congress, "owned politicians," to address our true economic problems. The key is forcing adherence to our Constitution . . . a brilliant document, which never intended a Federal Reserve or IRS.

Additional information can be found by reading *The Creature from Jekyll Island* by G. Edward Griffin or viewing Mike Rivero's "All Wars Are Bankers Wars," or Bill Still's "The Money Masters." My wife and I sat next to Bill at a "Project Freedom USA" Conference, organized by former and now deceased Congressman Jim Traficant and fellow patriot Jim Condit. Both were regular speakers at Freedompalooza. Traficant had courageously stood up to the IRS and succeeded in placing the burden of proof on the agency, rather than allowing for unconstitutional confiscation of taxpayer properties. Traficant subsequently came under attack by government powers, and his heartbreaking story is related in Michael Collins Piper's *Target: Traficant*. Project Freedom USA remains an important initiative advocating for an immediate end to the Fed and IRS, with implementation of a modest and fair consumption tax, instead.

Colorful and courageous James Traficant.

Government statistics reflect that U.S. unemployment has been fluctuating between 5 and 10% with inflation at nearly zero. ShadowStats.com more accurately reveals that unemployment is over 20% and inflation approximately 10%. This is not merely disconnect, but a gross manipulation of data by federal agencies in service to the banking establishment. It is no coincidence that senior bank officers and senior government officials play musical chairs—not in service to the American people, but to an increasingly corrupt system—for their collective aggrandizement.

America should return to a nationalist economic policy emphasizing ethical business practices and a true free market with limited government intrusion—conducive to the growth of entrepreneurship, small businesses, and the middle class—the backbone of America.

### TRADE

We should support "fair trade" as opposed to so-called "free trade" policies, which have led to the systematic deindustrialization of America. Until about 1970, Americans produced almost all of the products that they consumed. Unfair imports from Third World countries must be restricted, rather than facilitated, to permit domestic industries to once again compete. This can be accomplished through tariffs and quotas at home along with diplomatic pressure abroad. Under an "America First" system, the U.S. should withdraw from NAFTA, GATT, and the WTO and certainly not conclude new agreements, including the proposed Trans-Pacific Partnership (TPP). Manufacturing expertise and technology relies on a nation's ability to produce innovators and skilled workers, and it is the responsibility of our communities to develop a productive labor pool, rather than importing it from other countries, or offshoring production. A strong manufacturing base is absolutely necessary to sustain a world power.

So-called "free trade" has been the Trojan horse of multinational corporations in their ongoing and continuous fight against small businesses and the middle class. The concept of non-governmental organizations (NGOs) was invented by multi-nationalist academics as a means to increase their market share vis-à-vis small business.

Multinational corporations standardize manufacturing methods worldwide, whereby the costs of labor and regulation become the determining factors. By continuously moving manufacturing to the least regulated and lowest labor cost location, they are able to maximize profit and keep pricing just below small businesses' ability to compete.

America has run trade deficits for over 30 years; this is bad for the economy and devastating to our population, which now suffers from high unemployment and a stagnant economy. Fair trade is when the government institutes barriers to imports in order to allow domestic industry to compete.

NAFTA has been the worst agreement that United States government has entered into in its 240-year history. President Clinton enacted it as an executive order; it is not a treaty but a trade agreement. The result, as Ross Perot presciently put it, has been "the great sucking sound of American de-industrialization." In 1992, the U.S. had a trade surplus with Mexico of $5.7 billion annually. This surplus disappeared in the first year of enactment, turning into a deficit. The deficit grew every year for ten years and now stands at about $67 billion annually.

President George W. Bush was prodded by the NGOs to expand this disaster and enacted the Central American Free Trade Agreement (CAFTA), this time as a treaty to expand NAFTA to the entire Caribbean Basin, which includes Haiti, a nation with an average national per capita income of $400 per year—hardly comparable to American workers with their cost needs.

## FREE TRADE EXPANSION SINCE 2011

Not to be outdone with America's de-industrialization, President Obama and Congress expanded free trade to Colombia, Panama and South Korea in 2011. So what did we get from this? As Alabama Senator Jeff Sessions (one of America's true patriots) indicated, American domestic exports to Korea (between 2011 and 2014) only increased $0.8 billion (1.8%), while imports from Korea increased $12.6 billion (22.5%). Our trade deficit with Korea increased by $11.8 billion (80.4%), nearly doubling in three years. We have already lost more than 2.1 million manufacturing jobs to the Asian Pacific region since 2001. As former Nucor Steel Chairman Daniel DiMicco argued "We have not been engaged in free trade, but in unilateral trade disarmament and enablement of foreign mercantilism."

SEN. JEFF SESSIONS

The Trans-Pacific Partnership is being relentlessly promoted and President Obama wants Congress to approve fast-track legislation (Trade Promotion Authority) that would allow international trade and regulatory agreements to be expedited through Congress for the next six years without amendment. Fast track would ensure that these agreements—none of which has been made public—could pass with simple majority, rather than the 67 votes needed for treaties or 60 votes for legislative matters. Part of this treaty, which would supersede U.S. statutes, insures a backdoor for the flood of more immigrants into America.

Free trade treaties accelerate America's industrial decline and are supported by government policies, which favor multinational corporations. It would be wise to heed the words of Thomas Jefferson, who said, "Those nations that do not manufacture are the colony of those who do." What is blatantly apparent is that representatives of both major political parties serve these globalist interests and not their constituencies. The Republicrats will continue to answer to the multinational companies and their lobbyists at the altar of "free trade" until America becomes totally dependent upon foreign sources for everything. At that point we will become a colony of the producer nations. Until the American Revolution we were the colony of England, but after independence became a thriving manufacturing nation.

In general terms, America has utilized globalist negotiators for these trade and treaty negotiations. To turn this around, our contingency of negotiators should include American manufacturing executives of average-sized businesses with an America first loyalty.

## JOBS

America has programs (H-1B visa, for instance) which unbelievably take jobs from our own citizens and train foreigners to replace them. For example, currently Southern California utility employees are training their foreign replacements and must accept the company's terms if they are to receive severance packages. How can this happen, except by political and business betrayal?

And what is the purpose of the Department of Labor? What does it actually do with a budget of $13.3 billion? It should be disbanded. A disgusting and ironic effect of President Obama's policies is that 67% of black youth and 50% of Hispanic youth are now unemployed—minority groups which voted overwhelmingly for him.

America now has millions of unemployed, and millions more underemployed, which is what the Tea Party and Occupy movements are all about. The American people have been disenfranchised by the system and are rightfully angry at a government that is unable, or unwilling, to protect their interests. Our people need gainful employment, not treasonous economic policies. Not only have the last several administrations made incredibly bad decisions, but Congress has shown total ineptness.

For example, Senate and House banking committee chairmen Senator Chris Dodd (D-CT) and Congressman Barney Frank (D-MA) led a politically motivated and irrational change to our banking laws. This

Chris Dodd and Barney Frank.

allowed for people who had no assets, no down payment, and no possible way to repay a mortgage the ability to qualify for no-cash-down mortgages—and then force the banks to issue such instruments. It led to the crash of the entire mortgage industry. Scores of banking and insurance failures, and millions of foreclosures, along with the bankruptcies of Freddie Mac and Fannie Mae, resulted—with millions more foreclosures still anticipated due to ongoing job losses.

To create jobs, the current administration's solution has been to add 15% more federal employees, and America now has over two million of them. Of course, these are non-productive jobs and a further tax drain on America's working class. The lowest paid of these bureaucrats earns over double the average American income, and those in Washington D.C. earn over triple the average.

The Obama administration has also implemented an aggressive plan of bailing out states. This is not only irresponsible, but entirely beyond their constitutional authority. The bailouts by both President Bush and President Obama were initiated by borrowing money at interest. This brings both bailouts to over one trillion dollars, which our children and grandchildren will have to repay. The fact that much of this money was borrowed from foreign sources makes things even worse, as they will leverage for foreign policy decisions favorable to their interests. Borrowing money cannot reverse economic downturns, and increasing salaries for federal employees does nothing to stimulate the economy.

America needs manufacturing jobs desperately and the independence that comes with them. America has lost over 11.7 million manufacturing jobs and 57,000 small manufacturing businesses and production plants in the last 10 years, due to "free trade" policies which benefit the multinational corporations. We should not be isolationist, but must consider American protectionism and scrap these free trade agreements, replacing them with fair trade treaties.[1]

An economy that has a minimum wage of $7.25 or more cannot be labor competitive with nations that have no minimum wage and whose average income is $400 per year. While an average American laborer in manufacturing earns about $24 per hour, a Mexican laborer earns $3.12, and Mexico has no workers' compensation insurance, no Social Security co-pay, no labor unions, no pensions, no healthcare, and most importantly is not subject to American safety, environmental, or product liability laws, which add at least 15% more to product costs. And in foreign countries, there is often a willing and able police force to impose oppressive management edicts on workers. Is that to be imported to America, as well?

To resurrect American manufacturing we must shrink government and eliminate excessive regulations and taxes. Until our tax system can be totally restructured and the IRS dissolved, we must explore ways to encourage domestic business growth and entrepreneurship. This should include allowing for the repatriation of investment capital without penalty.

### TAXES

America currently has the most complex and confusing tax code in the entire world. Billions of man-hours are wasted filling out IRS forms. Our total tax code from the IRS includes 74,608 pages that you can purchase from the U.S. Government Printing Office. The fact that you need a staff of accountants and lawyers to try to figure out what the entire mess means is not included in the purchase price.

Laws written that cannot be understood form the seeds of tyranny. The operational management and payroll cost for the IRS is $11.7 billion. This system should have been scrapped decades ago and replaced with a simple and modest flat consumption (sales) tax.

American workers are now enslaved by excessive taxes, working to pay for unsustainable government largess. We must immediately and drastically cut government spending and end all programs which serve as wealth redistribution centers. The people should have the right to determine who will benefit from the fruits of their labor. We must free businesses and entrepreneurs to produce once again and shrink government back to within its constitutional limits.

Upon transitioning to a fair consumption tax, Treasury and Justice personnel should investigate true financial corruption. Trillions of dollars have been stolen from the American people by a banking cartel that controls the political landscape. Where fraud and other criminal banking activities have occurred, those responsible should not only be apprehended and prosecuted, but their enormous "ill-gotten" funds and assets (whether stored domestically or in foreign accounts) confiscated and restored to the U.S. Treasury.

## REGULATIONS

Today government's policy is that people and businesses must be constrained by good government. This premise is wrong. What government should do is only implement necessary (and constitutional) laws and regulations that support ethical actions, and not fine indiscriminately for violations of often badly written and poorly conceived laws.

Our national regulatory agencies are misdirected, inefficient, and invasive, and should be disbanded or reformed to better serve the public welfare. We must encourage American entrepreneurship and productivity, not stifle it with burdensome red tape and expense.

Not surprisingly, the U.S. leads the world in litigation. This does not benefit society or individuals and elevates costs for every product or service rendered. The costs, on average, are inflated by about 15% of base prices. The worst hit is manufacturing and medicine—and it has become common for manufacturers to move to foreign locations to avoid product liability suits or insurance costs.

## BUDGET

Congress and the executive branch have proven incapable of managing the nation's finances. The best way to solve that problem is with mandatory budget constraints and a balanced budget amendment—with no deficit spending allowed.

Each year, in increasing proportion, the federal government spends more than is collected in taxes, adding to our national debt, which now stands at nearly $18.3 trillion. When counting unfunded future liabilities, it is over $100 trillion.

This is unsustainable and an unfair burden to place on our progeny. Interest payments to the Federal Reserve banking cartel should be immediately repudiated as we take action to get our nation's finances in order.

We have come to a state in which government has become the answer and solution to all our woes. Sadly, government is never the answer; the answer lies in self-reliance of the citizenry, their character, and their independence. As any businessman will tell you, "Get the government out of my way and the economy will blossom." A great resource for business news is www.TheDailyBell.com.

CHAPTER NOTE:
1 "Monkey Business," Dr. Adrian Krieg, *The Nationalist Times*, October 2015.

THOMAS PAINE

## CHAPTER 14

# *Back to Nature*

"There are but two natural sources of wealth and strength:
the earth and the ocean." —THOMAS PAINE

I
N 2006, WE MOVED TO THE SMOKY MOUNTAIN region of Tennessee.
We had visited before and fell in love with its natural beauty and
central location in the eastern half of our country. It retains the
spirit of Americana, and is truly God's country. We soon met a
mountain legend, Casey Oakley, who has become a great friend. His
father was Wiley Oakley, the "Will Rogers" of the Smokies. Like his father, Casey is a spiritually inspired storyteller, and humorist. His father
had guided many dignitaries and, during the 1920s and 1930s, influenced the creation of the Great Smoky Mountains National Park.

Susan and me with Wiley "Casey" Oakley, Jr.

In America today, we are quickly eroding the natural wonders of our country. However, as our economy reveals, we must find ways to become productive again—but without spoiling our wonderful inheritance. Unfortunately, the environmental movement often stifles our productivity without protecting what is truly important.

## ENERGY

America's energy problems are not related to any lack of natural resources or inability to process product. Our problems with energy and the inordinately rising cost of energy products are based primarily on government energy policy and the effects from a misguided and overreaching environmental movement. The present administration's primary actions have led to increases of production in foreign nations to the detriment of domestic production.

Ethanol production, utilizing 138 million tons of corn, has driven the cost of food through the roof. Ethanol is a fuel that costs almost double that of diesel or gasoline production. We need our prime farmlands for agricultural use, so that we can eliminate America's dependency on foreign imports. America's small farmers have been virtually wiped out and most farmland is now held by agribusiness concerns. I helped create a motion picture about this, entitled "A Place to Grow." The soil is now dying, due to chemical fertilizers, herbicides, and pesticides, and organic family farmers are struggling to survive. This has largely been caused by a subsidized, and banker encouraged, industrialization of farming, aided by the Department of Agriculture. This department should be abolished, especially when they can spend $149 billion to regulate the cost of milk upwards, and provide subsidies to large corporate farmers while the small family farms are leveraged into poverty.

Washington's national energy initiative for green energy has failed. Solar energy production, which accounts for less than one percent of total consumption, has seen government-subsidized Solyndra and at least four other solar collector companies go bankrupt. Wind turbine programs have also been economic failures. Without massive tax credits, government subsidies for manufacturing companies, and huge tax rebates for users, no one would consider these alternatives for the private sector.

In the automotive industry, Elon Musk's Tesla, Solar City, and Space X companies receive nearly $5 billion in government subsidies. The IMF reports that total global energy subsidies are $5.3 trillion. The U.S. Department of Energy has no business spending taxpayer monies to incubate high-risk, high-tech companies. Musk, to his credit, admits the same—claiming that his companies don't need it to succeed. He also indicates that their subsidies are but a small pittance compared to the subsidies for the oil and gas industries.[1]

Fossil-based energy is finite. However, the Green position that we are running out of fossil (carbon)-based fuels is wrong. The United States has the world's second largest deposits of anthracite coal after South Africa. We have enough anthracite to meet all of our energy needs for the next 200 years, even if that were the only carbon-based fuel we used. Sasol is the world's largest coal liquefaction production facility. They have sales of $4.153 billion and employ 30,000 people in a large number of plants, which see to the fuel energy needs of the entire South African economy. We know that we can produce gasoline for about 40 cents per gallon utilizing the sequestration processes used by Sasol. So why is America importing oil and processed fuel, at four times the cost at which we can produce it? The answer lies largely with an international cartel of oil conglomerates, led by Rockefeller-associated banking interests.

North America has the largest natural gas, uranium, and oil deposits in the world. The consortium of petrochemical monoliths, along with environmentalists, have "purchased" a large number of U.S. politicians, and that is the primary reason why America's natural resources are controlled and not left for marketplace adjudication.

Major American oilfields, whose production has been blocked by environmental extremists, include the Beaufort Sea fields of Gull Island and Kuparuck, whose estimated reserves exceed that of Saudi Arabia, Kuwait, and Iraq combined. These fields are enormous (Kuparuck is 30 x 60 miles). Gull Island has not produced one dry well in an arc stretching over 40 miles. Shale oil and gas reserves in Rio Blanco County and at Stinking Water Creek, Colorado are realistically estimated at 1.5 trillion barrels—five times the entire oil reserves of Saudi Arabia! Fortunately, North Dakota (unlike many of our increasingly depressed states) is developing its Bakken crude fields, and experiencing a major oil boom. The fields, which have an estimated 413 billion barrels, are now producing 450,000 barrels a day and that number is expected to significantly increase.

We have sufficient energy potential in fossil fuel alone (in the ground in America) to see the country through the 23rd century without the slightest difficulty. As an aside, the Athabasca tar sands in Alberta, Canada cover 54,000 square miles and have an untapped reserve of two trillion barrels of oil, eight times that of Saudi Arabia.

The free market can and will develop the most efficient forms of energy. Government is not capable and should not be in the business of mandating to, or subsidizing, industries. If anything, the government should facilitate release of the large number of energy patents that have been suppressed and could revolutionize our lives with low-cost energy alternatives that are more environmentally safe. The Department of Energy should be disbanded.

## NATURAL ALTERNATIVES, NOT POISONS

Incorrect information has been disseminated about global warming and climate change. Basic tenants were unfounded, and based on old Soviet computer predictions. Even the UN climatic organizations have admitted that the computer-based projections are worthless. Much has to do with creating a "carbon tax" to help fund international programs that would destroy our national sovereignty, while imposing environment requirements on the American people.

Meanwhile, there are increasing numbers of substantiated reports of poisonous chemical spraying. "Chemtrails" are very real, containing aluminum, barium, and other heavy metals and chemicals—and not simply "vapor trails."

On several occasions, we have seen a checkerboard pattern of chemtrails over the Smoky Mountains, where normally there is little, if any, air traffic. In a short period of time, blue skies will turn white. It is not clear yet what the purpose of this concentrated spraying is, but it is being done without the knowledge or approval of the people, and with no mainstream reporting or official declaration. Noted geo-scientist Dr. Marvin Herndon has written, "The recent calls for open discussion of climate control or geoengineering tend to obscure the fact the world's military and civilian sectors have modified atmospheric conditions for many decades."[3] A great video on this topic entitled "Climate Engineering, Weather Warfare and the Collapse of Civilization" can be seen on YouTube.

Through the increasing use of genetically modified organisms ("GMO"s), our natural food chain is being replaced. GMOs are artificially manipulated in laboratories through genetic engineering. Testing and analysis have been less than satisfactory, yet companies such as Monsanto saturate the markets with their products, which are often later proven to be poisonous and otherwise unconscionably destructive. For over 100 years, they have successfully leveraged against their natural competitors in the marketplace, and escaped necessary criticism from the scientific community, or proper government scrutiny. Behemoths such as this company must be brought into accountability. The various regulative agencies (FDA, USDA, etc.) have not been responsible to the American people, and must be brought to task and redirected away from their unfair, and unconstitutional, suppression of organic family farmers—unless we subscribe to the philosophy of Henry Kissinger, who commented, "If you control the food supply, you control the people." For shocking information on the history of this company, see www.wakingtimes.com.

The American people are starting to realize that the medical and pharmaceutical industries do not always provide for our best health options. Natural remedies are proving to be far less costly and more effective than barbaric procedures and treatments, which often create a cascade of other health issues. Individuals have the unalienable rights to make decisions regarding their own bodies and government agencies and profit-seeking charlatans should never supersede this right. Efforts are increasing to legalize nature's medicine chest of cures, including cannabis and unreasonably controlled substances.

Medical marijuana advocate, Seth Green, centered behind large banner, with supporters. Seth suffers from MS and seizures and natural treatments are the most effective remedy.

CHAPTER NOTES:

1 "Elon Musk: If I cared about subsidies, I would have entered the oil and gas industry," *LA Times*, June 2, 2015.

2 "Respected Scientist Validates Public Concern Over Chemtrails," Mark Anderson, *American Free Press*, Sept 7, 2015.

JOHN ADAMS

# CHAPTER 15

# School Smarts

"Liberty cannot be preserved without general
knowledge among people." —JOHN ADAMS

## EDUCATION—NOT INDOCTRINATION

The same schools that once taught our children the knowledge, skills, culture, and traditions necessary to maintain and enhance our nation are now controlled by social engineers, cultural Marxists, and the Department of Education.

The following statement was found in the archives of the Carnegie Endowment:

> "The only way to maintain control of the population was to obtain control of education in the U.S. They realized this was a prodigious task [so] the portion of education which could be considered as domestically oriented [was] taken over by the Rockefeller Foundation and that portion which was oriented to International matters [was] taken over by the Carnegie Endowment."

The Rockefeller family (and by extension, global financial interests, including the Federal Reserve) supported the National Education Association, and powerful foundations (with private interests) continue to support the NEA and influence public policy. Many grants have been used to attack traditionalist education in favor of "scientific management" through standardized testing, rather than critical thinking. While per-student educational spending has more than

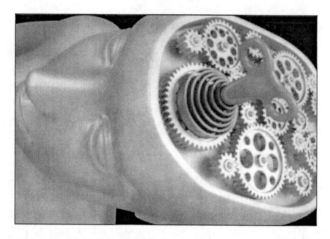

doubled since the 1960s, standardized test scores have continually fallen—social engineering at work.

Fortunately, a grassroots rebellion is underway and many parents are rejecting state-imposed tests and ill-advised programs such as No Child Left Behind and the more recent Common Core. Centralized government has no business in our local classrooms, nor do they have any constitutional authority. Parents and educators, through their school districts, should set curriculum and educational standards that meet their local area needs and not be subjected to invasive, costly and destructive government mandates.

"The ruling class has the schools and press under its thumb. This enables it to sway the emotions of the masses."

—ALBERT EINSTEIN

My wife has taught early childhood (pre-school through 3rd grade) throughout most of the last 40 years and the changes, which she has witnessed, have not been positive for our youth or country. Of particular distress has been the dissolution of the traditional two-parent family. Families are disintegrating due to destructive media and cultural influences, and non-productive government programs. Most teachers willingly accept the standard low pay, as they were inspired to educate and develop young minds when selecting their professions. That is the reward which the best teachers have always sought. I cannot help but insert a personal letter, which a former student recently sent to my wife:

"Hi, my name is _____, im fourteen now. Do you remember me? Well, I remember you. I was in your kindergarten and first grade class. I was the smart kid with trouble at home. My parents aren't very good people still, but I am no longer with them. There would be time I was very upset and you were always there to console me. You would talk with me, and make me smile.) I remember miss Peggy too, she was very kind to me to. When we would go to the back with her and count to 100 I would always go over, we would laugh and joke. I have always thought of you to be more than a teacher. You were like my best friend. I remember talking to the councilor and being afraid of what my parents would do to me, but you would talk to me and calm me down, making me smile. One day I stayed late after school because of the cops busting my parents for drugs. I met your husband, and you tried your best to help. Whenever something bad happened I would think of you, and what you tried to do. After I left that school, we moved a lot, in and out of foster care. My father got custody two years ago. He hated me, and didn't want me. I had to cook clean and care for him, my sister, and his girlfriend. He would beat me, it hurt bad but I would think of you and school and all of the happy times. It would go away. Well my nanny saved me, and now I live with her. My sister still lives with my father but he loves it, just her. He would never hurt her. I still have the picture that we took together making funny faces. My nanny asked who you were, I told her you are the best women in the world. I am doing very good in school, and I have done a lot of speeches about child abuse (I always talk about you), I even went to state with them. You [are] an inspiration to me and, I know, many others."

Today the best teachers are frustrated and leaving the profession. Government bureaucrats can never replace them.

Special education programs have also invaded the classroom, where special needs children are "mainstreamed," rather than having their needs met more effectively outside the regular classroom. This causes disruptions and lowers the level of learning for the rest of the class. Administering these programs costs school districts 25-34% of their budget allocations (for less than 10% of the students) due to government mandates. These mandated programs dictate how much time is to be spent on intervention, remediation, and physical programs—an impossibility without abandoning the needs of the other children.

Every community has an inalienable right to determine the educational program for their children. We should strongly support the states and their school districts' right to reclaim responsibility for educating their youth. Since the Department of Education was formed, the quality of American education has gone from 4th in the world to 34th. This is largely due to federal mandates, which have allowed government bureaucrats to hijack the classroom from district supervisors and classroom teachers. Most of the government programs have been social engineering experiments, which have lessened the quality of education and indoctrinated our youth away from traditional American values. The Department of Education wastes 70 cents of every tax dollar it receives for management and administrative overhead. It is invasive, costly, and ineffectual and should be abolished.

Although not a federal prerogative, we do encourage school districts to restore their schools to first-rate status. Teachers should emphasize traditional mathematics and literacy skills, which have practical application to everyday life. We encourage a full curriculum of American History to be taught to instill in our young people knowledge of and pride in the history, culture and heritage of the pioneers of the U.S., and not the poisonous cultural Marxist nonsense being fed to our children today. Organized classroom settings and well-disciplined learning environments should become the norm once again, as well as facilitating opportunities for alternative homeschooling arrangements and charter schools.

BENJAMIN FRANKLIN

# CHAPTER 16

# Social Issues

*"Be always at war with your vices, at peace with your neigh-
bors, and let each New Year find you a better man."*
—Dr. Benjamin Franklin

⚜

I N EVALUATING SOCIAL ISSUES and the funding of programs, we
should always keep in mind the constitutional limitations of
government and the freedom to choose by individuals. It is easy
to fall prey to socialist concepts, but as Margaret Thatcher famously said, "The problem with socialism is that you eventually run
out of other people's money."

## WELFARE NETWORK

Today there are nearly 50 million Americans getting food stamps
and 15 million getting unemployment benefits. We have millions on
welfare, in some cases third-generational welfare. And to top it off
we have nearly 30 million illegal immigrants seeking various forms
of assistance. This drain is wrong and unhealthy. We are denying our
people productive opportunities through poor policy, actually forcing them into poverty and government dependency. The answer does
not lay in government, but in freeing the private sector to produce
again.

Washington, D.C.'s falsely named "wars" (war on drugs, war on
terror, etc.) actually serve to grow those detriments. The "war on
poverty" has created a large and entrenched dependency class of citizens, and wastes trillions of dollars. Compassion should be based

on common sense, and charity should be the individual's domain, not a government reallocation of resources—by taking from some to give to others. We should phase out the "war on poverty" over a period of several years by moving those on welfare into a trade of their choosing with education and guidance. Thereafter, the entire program should be canceled and welfare needs left to the charity of individuals, communities, churches, and other organizations.

The federal government should have absolutely nothing to do with housing, including mortgage guaranteeing and incentive programs. The Department of Housing and Urban Development (HUD) should be eliminated. HUD has developed and expanded one slum after another in virtually every inner city and has created a dependency class, which is kept in poverty and ignorance. Their major utility is at election time—to be used as voting fodder for welfare-state advocates, who seldom leave office for the real working world.

## SOCIAL SECURITY

The greatest Ponzi scheme in the world is run by the federal government and is called Social Security. Americans who have been forced by the government to pay into this scheme have been cheated beyond most people's understanding. Unfortunately, various Social Security employees and government bureaucrats defend this system through gross misunderstandings and never-ending lies. When you ask Social Security to send you a statement of contributions, they list the money you paid in, but omit your employer's equal contribution on your behalf. So, before we even start, they cheated you out of 50% of the money collected on your behalf.

And nowhere, in any document that the government sends you, is there one penny of interest attributable to the tens of thousands, or hundreds of thousands of dollars that they collected on your behalf.

Most working contributors would collect several times the amounts that are actually paid them, were they to have invested those funds privately rather than through the Social Security System. And most unfairly, some people qualify for benefits who have never even contributed. Even Congress gets almost free healthcare, absolutely outrageous retirement benefits, 67 paid holidays and several weeks of vacation, unlimited sick days, free haircuts, free gym privileges, a special reserved dining room, $174,000 annual pay, and generous retirement provisions—yet they have the nerve to call the system citizens pay into a "benefit." By the way, several of our representatives are now calling for congressional pay raises.

Congress has removed the Social Security "safe," pilfered the contents and transferred them to the general fund—and then replaced the funds with dubious IOUs. If the system were run honestly there would be a surplus of funds in the trillions of dollars. This pilfering must stop.

## MEDICARE

The existing Medicare system is financially unsustainable. This is primarily due to the fact that medical costs have increased about 14% above that of the economy. A primary cause is Food and Drug Administration (FDA) mismanagement.

Regulations are not drawn up by Congress or a third party, but by agency insiders who increase their staffing and regulatory powers with each expansion of products regulated. They have constructed a draconian system for drug and instrument approval. For example, the FDA will not accept any foreign produced medication or instrument sale in America without the agency's direct approval and American domestic testing, although foreign testing is often more comprehensive and drug costs are much less. The average drug test for approval by the FDA costs the producer $14 million.

Over the last century, pharmaceutical companies gained a foothold in the medical industry by contributing to schools and programs with the caveat that they have an installed representative. In time, the pharmaceutical companies would introduce various drugs for testing, with sponsorship inducements and free samples to practitioners.

Eventually, training and procedures would favor drug treatment, rather than other natural, traditional treatments, and the number of schools offering holistic medicine would virtually disappear. Since then, the pharmaceutical companies have come to control medical practices and procedures, with severe scrutiny of any alternative treatments. Drug costs have since skyrocketed.

Not surprisingly, pharmaceutical campaign contributions to incumbent legislators are among the three greatest by classification, effecting FDA actions.

Individuals should not be denied their unalienable right to select their own healthcare and medical treatments, including natural remedies, and should not be forced to accept mandates from the medical establishment or pharmaceutical or insurance companies. Medicare costs should be dramatically reduced with severe penalties for fraud perpetrated by doctors, hospitals, and patients.

### HEALTHCARE INSURANCE

The Obama administration, with Democrat control of both houses, approved a 2,300 page takeover of the nation's healthcare industry—14.7% of the entire economy. They did this in the face of socialized medicine's failure in England, Russia and Germany, as well as most of Europe. Although Republicans regained control of the House in 2010, they have been unable or unwilling to make any effective changes to this draconian system.

Our present healthcare system is not efficient, but the proposed Obamacare is financially impossible to sustain, as well as being unconstitutional. There are various possibilities for providing health insurance, and free-market alternatives should be encouraged rather than submitting to forced and unworkable government solutions. Keep in mind that as more citizens return to productive jobs, the need for taxpayer assistance for healthcare will be reduced, with employer program options increasing.

Obamacare should be immediately repealed. The key to affordable healthcare resides with a free market that allows for a sufficient number of medical practitioners, and removes the cost-escalating practices of insurance companies, i.e., litigation—doctors, hospitals, equipment manufacturers, and pharmaceutical companies. It should discourage the current medical practices of conducting unnecessary testing and procedures, and allow for alternative means of healthcare, including natural remedies. Decisions should be the domain of individuals and their doctors, not government or the medical and pharmaceutical industries.

### FAMILY

Traditional family units have increasingly been targeted for destruction. Unfortunately, many American men and women are misplacing their priorities: Individualism and hyper-materialism have become more important than family and community. Millions of our youth have been coerced into a destructive Marxist, "politically correct" philosophy through television, radio, and print media. The exclusive groups that dominate these mass media outlets have methodically imposed a degenerate influence on our people.

We must encourage a return to a strengthened family unit as the norm for society. Alternative sexual lifestyles and violence should not be promoted by government policy or mass media, especially in public venues. The beliefs and sensitivities of majority parents should be respected and children not subjected to behavior deemed inappropriate in their communities. We must revitalize with the healthy, positive sense of community that we had shared for 200 years and, in the process, rekindle our spirituality and sense of charity. Get government out of our lives ... marriage and family are personal institutions and should not be subject to experimentation and control by social engineers.

## CRIME—TAKING BACK OUR COMMUNITIES

As the *NY Times* recently reported, "cities across the nation are seeing a startling rise in murders...."[1] America has become unrecognizably dangerous. The decline in the welfare and happiness of our people and nation has been marked by an acceptance of rampant crime as a way of life, as if we were actually incapable of curbing it. The American people should not have to worry about the legality of defending themselves, their families, homes, and possessions. Predators should not be given special rights at the expense of the safety and welfare of upstanding, law-abiding people.

At the same time, America's prisons are overcapacity and our per capita prison population exceeds all other nations, including the most tyrannical states. We have incarcerated many people for crimes which should not be classified as crimes—when no one was endangered and no harm done. If people make choices which may affect their personal health, but not others, then that is their personal decision and they should not be subject to a penal system that profits from their incarceration.

We should put common-sense principles into practice without delay: Enable police to concentrate on real criminals and serve the public welfare, not the political goals of the ruling elite. Enable Andy Griffith, not Darth Vader, to protect our communities.

**CHAPTER NOTE:**
1 "Murder Rates Rising Sharply in Many U.S. Cities," Monica Davey and Mitch Smith, *NY Times*, Sep. 1, 2015.

JAMES MADISON

# CHAPTER 17

# Immigration & Race

"[T]hose who acquire the rights of citizenship, without adding to the strength or wealth of the community, are not the people we are in want of." —JAMES MADISON

## IMMIGRATION

The best way to destroy a proud and strong nation is to radically alter its demographic make-up. Unbridled immigration is the quickest way to do that. With an influx of different ethnic groups, religions, languages, and customs, the traditional unifying elements are undermined. Today's diversity is transforming America into a "Tower of Babel" with no national unity or common respect. If diversity is to truly survive, then nations and regions must be able to retain their unique character and identity.

America traditionally welcomed strangers to her bosom. Those seeking a new life, free from oppression, were her lifeblood. Early immigrants were European derived and, due to their cultural similarities, were able to assimilate. However, heavy immigration in the late 1800s and early 1900s caused problems and eventually led to responsible immigration reform in 1924. These reforms saved this country from potential ruin and brought stability and profitability to America.

During the height of the civil rights movement in 1965, and in support of President Lyndon Johnson's "Great Society" experiments, Senators Jacob Javits and Ted Kennedy and Congressman Emanuel Celler ushered in immigration reform, which would destroy the order that we had achieved from 1924 on. Subsequent immigrants wouldn't hold the same level of respect for traditional American values and their admittance would not be merit based. They did not suit America's true needs, and were predominantly non-European. This would forever upset the American demographic and ultimately our economic stability and cultural cohesion. Contrary to socialists' interpretations, national homogeneity is key to a nation's strength, stability and long-term viability. The disingenuousness of the following quote is now apparent.

> "First, our cities will not be flooded with a million immigrants annually. Under the proposed bill, the present level of immigration remains substantially the same. . . . Secondly, the ethnic mix of this country will not be upset. . . . Contrary to the charges in some quarters, [the Immigration Act of 1965] will not inundate America with immigrants from any one country or area, or the most populated and deprived nations of Africa and Asia. . . . In the final analysis, the ethnic pattern of immigration under the proposed measure is not expected to change as sharply as the critics seem to think.... The bill will not flood our cities with immigrants. It will not upset the ethnic mix of our society. It will not relax the standards of admission. It will not cause American workers to lose their jobs."
>
> —SENATOR TED KENNEDY

In 1967, our population reached 200 million. In just 39 years after that milestone our population grew to over 300 million—a staggering increase of 100 million people, mostly due to immigration. With existing trends and no change to our immigration laws, the population is expected to top 400 million by 2043.[1] By the year 2042, the Census Bureau projects that European derived peoples will no longer be a majority of the population of the United States.[2] This is radical change—from over 90% European derived American to less than 50% in just 75 years. What will this do to the wealth of America and to the quality of life of our indigenous citizens? Productive American jobs will continue to disappear and we will take our seat in the theater of a global Third World. This is accelerated by our submission to NAFTA, GATT, and other trade agreements, which clearly do not favor the interests of America or its workers.

During 2006, at an immigration overpopulation conference held in Washington, D.C., the former governor of Colorado, Dick Lamm, silenced the huge audience with his eight points to destroy America. The audience realized that a methodical pluralist plan was quietly and pervasively destroying us and would not cease until immigration reform was enacted. Author Victor Davis Hanson, in his book *Mexifornia*, explains how immigration is destroying California and how it will roll across the country until it destroys all vestiges of the American Dream.[3] In LA County, according to the *Los Angeles Times*, 40% of all workers work for cash and do not pay taxes, 95% of warrants for murder are for illegal aliens, two-thirds of all births are to illegal aliens on Medi-Cal, paid for by taxpayers, nearly 60% of HUD property occupants are illegal, and of 10.2 million people only 5.1 million speak English.[4]

While many of these illegal immigrants are just seeking a better way of life, the quality of life of our existing population suffers and enforcement of our laws is made more difficult. Were we to protect our borders and guide other nations by our positive example, those nations would be inspired to better deal with their internal problems and alleviate many of the conditions that create discontent and exodus. Of great concern also in this age of increasing terrorism is the threat that we are allowing potential enemies to infiltrate us and bring their foreign allegiances into our communities. Moles can eas-

ily imbed themselves into communities when populations are in constant flux. Also, unquestionably, the drug trade has taken off due to cross-border operations by drug cartels and Hispanic gangs.

Unquestionably, America should immediately remove the incentives for illegal immigration. Birthright citizenship was intended for legitimate circumstances, not for pregnant mothers to sneak across our borders and have "anchor babies" to gain benefits and citizenship for their families. This must be ended, as must our federal government's demands that states and their hospitals pay for medical services to illegal immigrants and the education of their offspring. Illegal immigrant children currently can attend our schools without question, whereas American citizens must prove their eligibility and even provide proof of immunizations before they can attend any classes. Many government programs provide scholarship opportunities for illegals, and, at the same time, deny eligibility to our own citizens. We penalize our own people, while we encourage and reward illegals. Unbelievably, illegals can also collect Social Security benefits, even when they have never contributed.

Recent studies reveal that immigrant households access welfare at alarming rates, much higher than the native population (51% compared to 30%). This is true for new arrivals and long-time residents, as well as those with higher education levels—26% for college-educated immigrants, compared to 13% for college-educated natives.[5]

Why have certain forces been promoting immigration, both legal and illegal? Disloyal business interests may want to exploit cheap labor and avoid tax burdens. Others seek pluralism in America for their own reasons. Leo Pfeffer (former president of the American Jewish Congress), Norman Podhoretz (writer and member of the Council on Foreign Relations, or CFR), and organizations including the Jewish Federation, ACLU, and B'nai B'rith have all supported unrestricted open immigration.

According to Kevin MacDonald:

> "Reflecting the long Jewish opposition to the idea
> that immigration policy should be in the national in-
> terest, the economic welfare of American citizens was
> viewed as irrelevant; securing high levels of immigra-
> tion had become an end in itself."[6]

Barbara Spectre, an American-born Zionist, heads Paideia (the European Institute for Jewish Studies in Sweden), which receives funding from the Swedish government. She professes:

> "I think there's a resurgence of anti-Semitism because at this point in time Europe has not yet learned how to be multicultural. And I think we are going to be part of the throes of that transformation, which must take place. Europe is not going to be the monolithic societies that they once were in the last century. Jews are going to be at the center of that. It's a huge transformation for Europe to make. They are now going into a multicultural mode, and Jews will be resented because of our leading role. But without that leading role, and without that transformation, Europe will not survive."[7]

Barbara Spectre

With that transformation, Europe is being destroyed. The supremacism of people like Ms. Spectre is causing great resentment and the European people are wondering how outsiders can force change on their sovereign nations. And while the actions of people like Ms. Spectre, and treasonous politicians, defy logic, they meanwhile duplicitously support apartheid in Israel.

With the overriding actions of the European Union and pluralist organizations, their indigenous populations and historically distinct and progressive cultures are being systematically wiped out. Global elites are defying national architectures to unnaturally pit various ethnic, racial, religious, and cultural groups against each other. This is not by accident.

If one considers globalist plans for a New World Order, then the destruction of national sovereignty must weigh in. History has shown that no nation can survive any prolonged period of multiculturalism and multiracialism, especially when there no longer exists a common language, nor common values. Both the Democratic and Republican parties have been kicking the can of immigration down the street for years. All they have done is propose amnesty for millions of illegal aliens, which costs our nation and individual states billions of dollars annually and encourages more illegal invaders.

The vast majority of immigrants, both legal and illegal, now come from Third World nations in Latin America, Asia and Africa—lacking in education, science, art, law, governance, or industrial achievements in any way comparable to ours. Numerous studies have confirmed that there is no net economic benefit to the U.S. economy from Third World immigration due to the added costs of education, infrastructure, healthcare, welfare programs, and law enforcement. Statistically, a largely disproportionate number of crimes are committed by illegal immigrants.

We should immediately: deport all illegal and criminal aliens; impose massive penalties for employing them (require E-Verify when hiring); end the H-1B Visa program which is replacing American workers with foreign workers (approximately 1 million per year); utilize the U.S. military for border security; repeal the Immigration Act of 1965, placing a moratorium on all immigration until responsible reform can be legislated; stop advantaging immigrant populations over our own citizens by ending legislative mandates that require states to provide health, education, and employment benefits (while denying states the ability to enforce existing legislation designed to prevent illegal entry); and eliminate birthright citizenship, chain migration and asylum.

The character of a nation depends on those who comprise it. A country is the product of its people; if you radically change the people you also radically change the character of the country. The citizens of a nation have the right to protect their sovereign identity and way of life.

## RACE

Racial demographics are one of the primary determinants of a nation's character. America's Founding Fathers were European derived and this country was settled and built through their efforts and that of their progeny. Less than 50 years ago our nation was 90% white, with approximately 10% black, and a very small representation of other races. Since then, we have been undermined by internationalists seeking to destroy the "heritage, traditions and identity" of America with a flood of impoverished Third World immigrants, both legal and illegal. We are now approximately 65% white, 14% black, 15% Hispanic, and a small percent Asian.

This is bizarre and not happening by accident. During the 20th century, socialist global elites hijacked American institutions and media, and began indoctrinating our people into accepting "Cultural Marxism"—or as it's euphemistically known, "political correctness."

> "We (Jews) must realize that our party's most powerful weapon is racial tensions. By propounding into the consciousness of the dark races that for centuries they have been oppressed by Whites, we can mold them to the program of the Communist Party. In America we will aim for subtle victory. While inflaming the Negro minority against the Whites, we will endeavor to instill in the Whites a guilt complex for their exploitation of the Negroes. We will aid the Negroes to rise in prominence in every walk of life, in the professions and in the world of sports and entertainment. With this prestige, the Negro will be able to intermarry with the Whites and begin a process which will deliver America to our cause."
> —ISRAEL COHEN, *A Racial Program for the Twentieth Century*, 1912. Also in the Congressional Record, Vol. 103, p. 8559, June 7, 1957

There are several "elitist" groups fomenting racial animosities, as part of a divide and conquer strategy to transform America. Organizations like the Southern Poverty Law Center (SPLC), the Anti-

Defamation League (ADL), and the Jewish-founded National Association for the Advancement of Colored People (NAACP). These organizations and countless others would begin systematic legal challenges to America's existing social norms and begin a process of cultural division.

These groups are usually well funded and, as with the SPLC, hold lucrative government contracts—generally based on propaganda, greatly exaggerating the power and influence of so-called "hate groups." The mainstream media reinforces their distortion of events and facts. Many of the targeted groups are actually led by agents provocateur, some insidiously working for the government and others for these organizations. As Lenin said, *"The best way to overcome the opposition is to lead it."* It can then be led off the cliff.

In years past, slavery and indentured servitude were abominations, and discrimination should not have been allowed, but to now institutionalize prejudicial actions against majority interests is equally injurious. Affirmative action programs are a form of government-imposed discrimination. They are unfair and unconstitutional, and the most qualified people are often denied just opportunity. It is time to end quotas and discriminatory "affirmative action" programs . . . "equal rights for all citizens, special privileges for none."

Lloyd Miller, in white, with family at his retirement.

Within my own family, my father was ultimately denied promotion to Captain on the Des Moines (Iowa) Fire Department, due to racial quotas. He was hard working, reliable and highly qualified, but affirmative action quotas elevated less qualified minority candidates to be promoted ahead of him. The results were that my father retired early and 2 of the 3 benefiting minority candidates ultimately failed, because they were not qualified or prepared for advancement. This caused not only safety concerns and inefficiencies, but also unnecessary resentments.

Minority citizens and their families have not really benefited from these programs as they are suffering from vast changes in the traditional fabric of American society, and jobs are currently being taken by illegal immigrants. Also drug use and crime have become epidemic, and the government has undermined the role of the father and husband (currently, over 71% of Black children are born out of wedlock). It is more profitable for the male to not be in the household, leading to new generations growing up without a normal and healthy family life, but rather with dependencies on gangs or government agencies.

A healthy sense of pride has been adversely affected through welfare assistance programs and by the loss of decent paying jobs. Rather than aiding families, government has provided crutches which lead to their dissolution. It is time to restore self-pride in all of our communities by promoting new opportunities through productive jobs.

**CHAPTER NOTES:**

1 "US Population Passes 300 Million Mark," Stephen Ohlemacher, Associated Press, October, 17, 2006.

2 MacDonald, p. 296.

3 *Mexifornia*, Victor Davis Hanson

4 *Los Angeles Times*, Monday, September 18, 2006.

5 "New Report: 51% of Immigrant Households Access Welfare," Marguerite Telford, Center for Immigration Studies, Sep. 2, 2015.

6 MacDonald, p. 296.

7 Interview with Israeli IBA News, 2010, distributed on You Tube.

"Here's freedom to him who would speak.
Here's freedom to him who would write.
For there's none ever feared that the truth
should be heard, save him whom the truth
would indict." —ROBERT BURNS

# CHAPTER 18

# Cultural Marxism vs. Walt Disney

"We are never in a proper condition of doing justice
to others, while we continue under the influence of
some leading partiality."     —THOMAS PAINE

⚜

## CULTURAL MARXISM

I often ask, "Where have our heroes gone?" At one time, we could
find them among us, always visible when danger appeared. They
were bigger than life, incredible looking, noble-minded and respectful of all that was good and decent. They were part of a
world that honored beauty, skill, and fair play.

I also ask, "Where are the good stories?" At one time, we could
discern right from wrong because stories promoted truth, justice, liberty, and peace. The world felt good when they ended happily, or inspired us to overcome when they did not. They made us want to be
better people and live in a better world.

At one time, we lived in hope that the American dream was possible, that we could achieve greatness and find peace, love, and happiness. The dream required hard work, honesty, and humility, but it
was within reach. Our Founding Fathers and ancestors proved it
could become real.

Cultural Marxism, a radical communist philosophy based on the
teachings of Karl Marx, has been killing our heroes, our stories, our
dream—and all else that we have worshiped and believed in. Employing critical theory to attack traditional institutions and values,
several movements would grow to undermine American values and

demographic interests through the infiltration of our schools, media, and government. The communist-centric "Frankfurt School," the "Fabian" socialists, the "Boas" anthropology movement, Darwinism, and the promotion of Freudian theories would all attack the conservative American belief system and break apart the family unit. Even our vocabulary has undergone radical transformation to alter meanings and impart criticism of traditional interpretations and ideals. But these ideals are not quite dead. Our heroes and stories can rise from the ash heap. The American dream can be restored, if we will only fight for it!

There are several leaders in this fight, most notably E. Michael Jones who publishes *Culture Wars*. I first met Mike at a conference in Tehran where he gave an incredible, fact-filled presentation. He clearly demonstrated how an orchestrated program to destroy organized religions and family values is at work.

Jones also showed how the feminist movement has served, not to free women,

Karl Marx

but to sexually exploit them and pit the sexes against each other. This is repetitively done in media and through political actions by attacking traditional paternal role models and denigrating females who might abandon careers to raise and educate their children. Compounding this assault, two wage earners are now required to support a family that one wage earner could previously.

Same-sex marriage is a recent, abnormal transformation of the societal norm of a man and woman joining in marriage (usually with spiritual or religious foundations, to procreate and raise a family).

1960s-70s radical feminists—Bella Abzug, Betty Friedan, Gloria Steinem

What people choose to do in their personal lives is their own business, but government should not be involved in sanctifying or adjudicating personal relationships. Government has only entered this discussion for money and control—through creation of arbitrary and unconstitutional tax laws with discriminating benefits. If these parasitic money manipulations were eliminated, then government could (and should) leave the defining of relationships to the individuals involved.

> "No matter what the majority wanted, the minority prevailed, thanks to a Supreme Court whose dictates were never defied by a Christian majority."  —PAT BUCHANAN

Another champion of the truths to our cultural enslavement is Dr. Kevin MacDonald, author of *Culture of Critique* and publisher of *The Occidental Observer*. He has statistically reported on Jewish control of motion pictures and other forms of mass media as they influence public beliefs and attitudes to redefine our culture. MacDonald's book reflects estimates of Jews controlling over 40% of the general fields of mass media, high finance, legal, intellectual elite, and entertainment.[1] I personally believe those estimates to be low, especially when considering the consolidated degree of influence they have on specific and critical areas. When a unique group of people comprises less than 2-1/2 percent of the population, yet control powerful industries, questions should be asked. Were it any other group with this kind of disproportionate representation, the Jewish community would demand it.

To do business in Hollywood, one must play by unwritten and unspoken rules, but rules nonetheless. The first and foremost rule is to always support the Jewish-Zionist agenda. Their definitions of political correctness are usually anathema to traditional American values, and this destructive reality has been well hidden, but is increasingly coming to be recognized.

My career choice was to produce quality motion pictures—entertainment that goes beyond satisfying our fickle emotions, but that speaks truths and touches our very souls to inspire us to take positive actions. I was fortunate to become a part of the motion picture industry, not realizing that I had truly entered Alice's Wonderland.

Hollywood insidiously propagandizes us to believe non-truths, to worship anti-heroes, and to acquiesce to a world of increasing decadence and despair—a New World Order. Independent alternatives are faced with an insurmountable task to take on the Hollywood juggernaut. But it should be a simple matter of developing, producing, and marketing one quality motion picture at a time. In so doing, we could tap the spirit of the people by inventively reaching out to them. They are a Sleeping Beauty, put to sleep by the poisons of our enemy, and need a Prince Charming to wake them and give them life again.

As you by now know, Walt Disney was my idol growing up, and I still long for that Davy Crockett coonskin cap. Walt was a multi-talented genius who was faced with many personal and business challenges throughout his lifetime, but he always overcame them. Today, he would have great difficulty.

### WALT DISNEY

"All the adversity I've had in my life, all my troubles and obstacles, have strengthened me... You may not realize it when it happens, but a kick in the teeth may be the best thing in the world for you." —WALT DISNEY

Walt Disney was an American icon who personified the best of America with his films, television shows, and theme parks. He represented beauty, kindness, and inspiration to an increasingly troubled world, and his fatherly presence brought comfort and joy to our lives. If there can be any true measure of positive human achievement in the 20th century, then Walt Disney, an entrepreneur of unparalleled creative genius, would surely go down as the greatest force in entertainment.

Generations have been impacted by his heartwarming and classic works and by the positive and innovative examples he set. He was my idol and had fate delivered me to his era, I would have been at his doorstep, seeking his mentorship, in service to his world. But it was not to be, for I was still a kid when he died. Although I worked a few years later as an usher in a theater that always played the Disney films, I knew that the magic had died, too.

While Walt's name nostalgically lingers on, the company that he built has largely abandoned the principles and values that he stood for, and has instead joined the ranks of Hollywood's materialistic purveyors of crass and decadent entertainment. Each year there are fewer exceptions to this disturbing reality. Walt would be more than disappointed, but not surprised. He knew his enemies and their insatiable appetite for subverting the dreams of others. But Walt left us an incredible legacy of stories, characters, and wonderworks—and challenged us to make this a better world. Accordingly, he developed five guiding principles to make dreams come true: think tomorrow, free the imagination, strive for lasting quality, have stick-to-it-ivity, and have fun.

WALT DISNEY

Walt was born December 5th, 1901, before the creation of the Federal Reserve, and the IRS, and before the numbering of wars. Walt's father was Irish-Canadian and his mother German-American. Life was not easy for the Disney family, and they relocated as job opportunities dictated. But growing up in the Midwest shaped Walt's values and gave him an Americana, "Pollyanna" perspective. His formative years were spent in Marceline, Missouri, and many of his later inspirations came from those simple but wonderful experiences of living near "Mainstreet," but also near fields and forests, rivers and trains— and farm animals. It was there that his love for drawing began.

During WWI, Walt tried to enlist but was still a minor, so he joined the Red Cross as an ambulance driver, serving in France. Upon his return, he went to Kansas City, where he worked as a commercial artist. There he improved his cartooning skills, met other artists and formed his own ventures—producing live-action and animated shorts. After limited successes and failures, Walt eventually migrated to Hollywood, partnering with his brother, Roy, and his friend, Ub Iwerks. The next several years were tumultuous and his successes did not come easy. His short films were very popular, but distributors cheated him on returns and even stole his characters and, at times, his animators. Walt struggled throughout his career, but especially during those early years.

Many people falsely think that the motion picture industry was a Jewish creation. In actuality, Thomas Edison was the inventor of the motion picture camera and through his "Trust" began to organize the burgeoning new business. Creative directors, exemplified by D. W. Griffith, captured the public's fascination with quality films and the future looked bright. Jewish merchants, recognizing the potential, scrambled for a piece of the action and became notorious for circumventing payments to the Trust. Through their Nickelodeon theaters, they built their own distribution networks and grew rapidly by showing racy, exploitative material. They moved production to Hollywood, primarily to escape paying royalties to Edison's Trust. In time, and with felonious tactics, they prevailed but did not yet have a stranglehold on the industry.

Walt's big break came with the creation of Mickey Mouse in 1928, after which his independence, and fame, steadily grew. No longer trusting the New York or Hollywood distributors, he learned to negotiate less larcenous agreements. However, his company would not gain true independence until developing its own marketing and distribution capabilities, many years later.

As his company grew, Walt pioneered as no other—pursuing perfection and innovation, rather than just going for the "quick bucks," as most Hollywood studios did. His breakthroughs included producing the first sound animation, the first color animation, and the first feature-length animation. His quality was unmatched and the public went crazy for his films—and he won unparalleled accolades and awards.

By the "golden era," Walt Disney Studios was the only major motion picture company that was not Jewish owned or controlled and Walt believed that he was consistently discriminated against. Hours after the bombing of Pearl Harbor, his studio was occupied by the U.S. Army. No other studio was singled out this way. During the war, Walt, as a true patriot, made numerous films for the government's propaganda campaign, at great financial loss to the studio. Yet Secretary of the Treasury Henry Morgenthau was never satisfied. During these years, the other studios profited greatly by making substandard films that the public desperately needed for diversion. Disney was forced to go several million dollars in the red and by war's end was on the verge of bankruptcy. Then another studio chief offered to fund the millions Walt needed for his next two animated features, but only if Walt agreed to sell out his operation. Furious, Walt resisted and survived. Fortunately, his post WWII features were enormously successful, aided by the eventual freeing up of European currencies.[2]

After the war years, Walt felt persecuted by communist and union activists and became suspect of his competitors. According to Leonard Mosley, "He didn't trust Jews, no matter what their proclaimed political affiliations."[3] Walt was a Christian patriot and an anti-communist, who helped found the Motion Picture Alliance for the Preservation of American Ideals. As a man of principle, he resisted unfair business tactics and what he perceived as coordinated attacks against his company, and our nation.

In actuality, Walt sought the best talent he could for his projects, and gave career opportunities to many aspiring artists. He was not averse to hiring Jewish artists (writers, actors, composers, etc.) and treated each person as an individual, on their own merits. Walt was beloved by most of his employees, who were inspired to create greater quality than possible anywhere else—and they were honored to be on his special team. As an idealist, and an honorable man, he would fight for "right," in an industry not noted for its integrity or fair play. He was foremost an American patriot, who put God, country, and family first.

The 1950s were a great decade for Walt Disney. He ventured into television as a way to help fund his Disneyland theme park vision and further market his company name. Disney programs took ABC from a small upstart to a major network with a wonderful mix of family entertainment. Hundreds of educational and outdoor adventures captured the imagination of home audiences, and top-rated series, such as "Davy Crockett," "The Mickey Mouse Club," and "Zorro," became enormously successful merchandising franchises. Walt's affection for the spirit of our Founding Fathers came through with countless patriotic shows about freedom: "Johnny Tremain," "The Scarecrow of Romney Marsh," "Tales of Texas John Slaughter," "The Nine Lives of Elfego Baca," "Swamp Fox," and many others.

Some of Disney's classic motion pictures and a few of the 1950s-60s television series can be acquired on DVD, but the current company management releases them in very limited quantities, which sell out immediately and then command huge prices in the aftermarkets. What a shame, as these programs are so much better than contemporary programming and could have a positive impact on our youth, if marketed more broadly to the television and video markets.

Many people view "Disneyland" as Walt's crowning achievement. Opening in 1955, it took the world by storm—as "the happiest place on Earth." However, it was only the beginning of his theme park visions, most of which were never realized due to his untimely death on December 15, 1966. He died abruptly from lung cancer, at the age of 65, before having properly developed a capable successor. Walt had so many projects still in the works and so much creativity remaining that we can only wonder what other amazing visions this great man might have brought to life, had he only had a few more years.

Unfortunately, if other Walt Disneys now try to rise, the industry will suppress them. Today, Hollywood is all about insider packaging and promoting a destructive agenda, not about developing quality, real talent, or new visions. Instead of being inspired to greatness, we are being dumbed down and propagandized to accept the values of Mammon. Hollywood and the media, in general, now serve a sinister purpose of controlling the masses and reducing us, almost to an animal state. They have largely succeeded, but as long as the memory of visionaries like Walt Disney live on, we can have role models for a very different future—one in which we can enjoy life and each other and achieve great things... our American dreams.

Some people believe that Walt Disney was cryogenically frozen—and will be restored to life one day, when medical science can achieve such things. It is an appropriate myth, as Walt believed that almost

Cover of the March/April 2011 issue of THE BARNES REVIEW magazine.

anything was possible, and we certainly could use his genius today. But the family denies it. When Walt did pass on, his brother Roy took over for a few years and oversaw the opening of Florida's "Walt Disney World." Roy was succeeded by company faithful Card Walker, and eventually by Walt's son-in-law, Ron Miller.

Unknown to most people, Walt fought his entire career to build his dream, against incredible odds—and he succeeded! Unfortunately, after his death, the company floundered, finally succumbing to his enemies. I was in Hollywood at these later critical junctures, gaining some unique insights.

In early 1980, as I prepared to leave military service, I wrote Ron Miller, seeking an opportunity to work for the company. He had Frank Paris write back a courteous but dismissive letter. I learned later that Ron was having his own difficulties and a battle was brewing on the board of directors between Ron and Roy Jr. Their animosities were long-held and Walt's greatest failure was in not finding or developing a long-term successor with the necessary creative vision and management ability. Given Walt's special qualities, it would have been difficult to find an acceptable replacement, if not impossible—and death simply took him too suddenly. Roy Jr., as the only son of Walt's brother, eventually became the largest individual stockholder, as Walt's shares were divided among his wife, Lillian, and their two daughters, Diane (Ron's wife) and Sharon. Unfortunately, the family animosities would grow—perhaps being manipulated by outside forces.

When I reached Hollywood in 1983, as a USC graduate student, I learned that Tom Wilhite was president of production and working for Ron Miller. Tom had gained quick promotion by heading up the marketing for Mickey Mouse's 50th anniversary celebration tour—a unique success for an increasingly desperate company. I was able to get to know Tom through contacts from our home state of Iowa. He was to become a key figure during the takeover of Disney in 1984. In late 1983, Tom came to screen a new Disney release for my USC class and, through his comments, the difficulties at Disney became publicly apparent.

The next summer, I was disappointed to intern at Paramount, rather than at Disney, but ironically, the team that I worked for (Michael Eisner, Jeff Katzenberg, et al.) left Paramount shortly thereafter to take over Disney. Roy Jr., working with his partner, Stanley Gold, had finally succeeded in convincing enough of the Disney family members and other stockholders to oust Ron Miller and bring in a key part of the Paramount team, which quickly fired hundreds of the Disney faithful to bring in their own. Tom was given an extremely generous severance (as he indicated in the "trades") and later formed his own production company, Hyperion Pictures, which thereafter made a score of unmemorable films. My connections to the Paramount team and the remnants of the Disney team led to no personal opportunities, as the Disney label was about to go through a Hollywoodization process that would not involve people with Midwestern values or Walt Disney loyalties.

During the next few years, the new management team would not show any exceptional artistic ability, but they were shrewd business people and recognized the value of the Disney name and library. They very successfully began to re-release Disney's classic motion pictures, and grew a chain of Disney stores to capitalize on various merchandizing possibilities. The Disney Channel finally took off and company balance sheets reversed direction. These successes enabled the new team to increase their ownership positions in the overall company and stockholders were once again happy, as their dormant gold mine had been re-tapped. Productions would gradually increase and efforts were made to seemingly meet traditional Disney programming expectations. In succeeding years, however, the quality would stealthily subside to the level of the other major studios and Americana would lose its representative voice.

In 1989, I last saw Tom, then Director at the Sundance Film Festival, but gained no new insights. By 1993, I left Hollywood with its elusive deal making to try to build my own independent opportunities. To succeed in Hollywood, you must be willing to abandon the values of Americana. That was a compromise that Walt would never make and is a compromise that has since been destroying the moral fiber of our country. Since the takeover of Disney by Hollywood's elite, there has been a gradual emasculation of Prince Charming and de-feminization of Sleeping Beauty. Cynicism has replaced charm, and nature's normal roles have been turned upside down through an advocacy of alternative lifestyles, miscegenation, and contempt for Christian or traditional American values.

During the early 1990s, I visited Walt Disney's hometown in Marceline, MO and got to know Kaye Malins and her father, Rush Johnson—who had been friends with Walt and Roy. The town has a Walt Disney Museum and other special tributes, yet retains its small-town qualities. Ironically, the place in which he spent only a few years now gives him greater homage than Hollywood, or even his own company.

The Disney empire is all about money now, and the not-so-subtle subversion of Walt's world. Contemporary films, television shows, music productions, and merchandise are increasingly abhorrent to a healthy culture. Walt would be shocked to learn that his theme parks are no longer exclusive havens for families, but have become temples for political correctness and Cultural Marxism. They now tolerate, if not promote, open demonstrations of alternative lifestyles and perversions that Walt would have clearly rejected.

Faced with the present-day world, Walt would be dismayed—but I believe he would still be the optimist. As one who always brought dreams to life, he would be leading the charge to reclaim our country and the future of our progeny. With quality entertainment as his primary weapon, he would restore the American dream.

CHAPTER NOTES:
1 MacDonald, p. 305.
2 *Disney's World*, Leonard Mosley, pp. 204-207.
3 *Ibid.*, p. 221.

BEN STEIN

# CHAPTER 19

# Hollywood & Motion Pictures

"Do Jews run Hollywood?
You bet they do, and what of it?"
—BEN STEIN

I was fortunate to enter the University of Southern California's Peter Stark Motion Picture Producing Program. It is a prestigious program designed to develop major producers and studio executives. The director of the program, Art Murphy, was a former naval commander and a curmudgeon. In his own way, he recognized the challenges ahead and uniquely gave me an opportunity. Art was a noted film critic and industry analyst, who accepted me into his program, whereas other pundits often revile someone with my background to seek only those with industry connections. At the start of the program, Art said that it was a Jewish business, but anyone had the potential to succeed. I think that were he alive today, he would further condition that statement.

Out of the 20 of us who graduated in my class, 5 were Jewish. Most have been quite successful, producing major motion pictures and television shows. A few are good; most are not. Many are outwardly disrespectful of Christian and traditional American values, and their impact has been significant.

Although uniquely trained and qualified, almost all of our remaining classmates would eventually leave the industry to support themselves in other professions. Why? In my opinion, there is an overwhelming and unrelenting tide that shapes the development, production, and marketing of content, and the corresponding em-

As a USC "Peter Stark" graduate student.

ployment opportunities. This tide holds Jewish-Zionist interests foremost and it is according to their unspoken and unwritten rules that content is guided and success enabled or disabled.

Upon graduation I would have liked to join Disney, but the company was not the same since Walt died and I had no advocates. My experiences interning at Paramount revealed how paranoid the staffers were. Nepotism reigned and the lot was full of arrogant "executives," "stars," "deal makers," and lackeys. It seemed to me that a lot of self-absorbed and irresponsible people were defining our "pop culture" and this did not bode well for the future of entertainment or the morality of our youth. I tried to pitch a few story ideas to obtain "development deals" (project funding), but there was no interest. Deals were being made based on insider relationships rather than merit.

I wanted to influence society in a positive way and become like my idol, Walt Disney, and legendary filmmakers John Ford, Frank Capra, George Stevens, and David Lean. A contemporary great is Ridley Scott. He usually makes thought provoking films, "Gladiator" being my favorite. Unfortunately, there are few filmmakers today who consistently make quality, and without a Walt Disney to mentor me in the flesh, I decided my best course of action would be to pur-

With daughter, Amanda, next to Program Director Art "A.D." Murphy and flanked by classmates mega-producer Neal Moritz, and Harvey Grossman

sue independent production work on low-budget films and gain "trench warfare" experience.

This is a great way to learn, but a painful way to live. There is no money in it and you are forced to wear numerous hats. Most of the other people at this level of production are also hungry and few have any idea how to produce quality. Independent producers are always looking for money to fund their films. They don't usually get it from the major studios, so they look elsewhere. Some will go into personal debt and some will scour for support from friends, family, and others. The majority will never get a film off the ground but those who do are convinced they are making the next blockbuster and will soon be welcomed onto the studio lot. They don't realize that the studios view them as hopeless wannabes, who are not entitled. The tenacious hopefuls who do find a way to make a film are forced to make incredible production compromises because they are working with "chump change," rather than millions of dollars of industry funds. However, compared to the garbage coming out of Hollywood, many independent features are more meriting of national release.

During the next several years, I worked as line producer or assistant director on mostly poor quality films, which appealed to the exploitation markets. They were horror films or seedy action films that were deserving of an "R" rating and limited audiences. Independent filmmakers pursue these kinds of motion pictures, as the studios usually cede those markets to them. Many people think that future filmmaking stars are independents who make great films that are recognized at film festivals. In my opinion, that is not the case. The few independents who do succeed generally make the most shocking films, which condemn traditional values. They are the ones embraced by Hollywood, while those that aspire to quality usually linger on the vine.

Regarding festival finds—a studio might not justify spending $50 million for an executive's nephew to make a bizarre film for the studio (although they increasingly do). But if the nephew gets his film made independently, it will often be accepted by a major film festival, where quality independent films are routinely rejected, and surprisingly win a major award. Whether it has anything to do with studio sponsorship of the festival or relationships is only speculation. But with a festival-winning film, the executive can now justify his studio picking up his nephew's bizarre creation and sharing it with the "deserving public." The hype that attends these kind of films can often make successes of them—although the more discerning public is shaking their heads wondering how anyone could see it as a good film. No matter. A few critics will and now the filmmaker is off to a stellar career with the studios—and through media induced peer pressure, an increasingly fickle audience will accept it as "good filmmaking."

Now, for those filmmakers who make quality, and I've seen many of them at less industry supported festivals, they are left with a film that will not gain a distributor. The exception is low-level distributors (I call "bottom feeders"), who serve the small exploitation markets and live off of desperate filmmakers. Quality films cannot make money serving the exploitation markets and any money that might be made will be taken off the top for distribution fees and expenses. Also, a small distributor may have his own film that is a dog, but somehow it sells for more money than the quality film. (I call this "relationship packaging.") And we won't talk about creative accounting.

With all of this you might wonder why any noble-minded independent would even try against such odds. The reason is they want to fulfill their American dream, which is increasingly being limited to the Hollywood elite and their sycophants. Any discussion of nepotism, cronyism, or racism is immediately dismissed in Hollywood, especially since there are select representatives of different races and cultural persuasions who are allowed success. Others pursue their trade in ways which promote Hollywood's "world values," thus allowing for their individual successes and society's demise. Therein lies the Hollywood game.

Does Hollywood have an agenda? Industry defenders would scream, "No." However, among many independents, it's assumed that if you want to make a film and be assured of marketing, you must make one which attacks Christianity or challenges traditional standards of decency, or which edifies the Holocaust. Michael Medved, in his book *Hollywood vs. America*, dealt with Hollywood's war against traditional values and cites examples of how much more profitable "G," "PG," and "PG-13" films are than "R" rated films— yet more "R" rated films are released each year than all others combined.[1] If responsibility or pride of quality didn't matter to the studios, you'd think that profitability would. However, when one can control the content released to the public and overwhelm them repeatedly with an altered set of values (employing peer pressure tactics), then perhaps there are other goals.

Since the early days of filmmaking, the major studios have tried to restrict competition. They went to Hollywood to escape paying Edison for his patents and have played by their own rules ever since. There have been times of governmental regulation. The Hays Commission regulated content until the mid-1960s, when the Motion Picture Association of America (MPAA) was formed to self-regulate content through its ratings administration. The MPAA is made up of the major studios as member companies and has become an important lobbyist/representative in Washington, D.C. for the interests of Hollywood's major players. In my opinion, its formation has helped lead to the disintegration of societal standards of decency.

The motion picture industry has often been accused of anti-trust violations. This usually concerns "vertical integration," whereby the handful of major studios produce and distribute films and own theaters (as well as cable and TV channels), thereby restricting competition. Since the Paramount consent decrees of 1947 and the studio's subsequent divestiture of theater ownership, the government rules of ownership have eased considerably. The studios may no longer be in strict violation of the Sherman Antitrust laws, but they have certainly found coercive ways to restrict competition. Today, the industry majors are actively consolidating and consuming smaller companies that might pose a challenge to their markets. It has become prohibitively costly to enter the business at a level of true competition in the global marketplace. The American majors have gone international and formed partnerships and ownership interests in most foreign markets. What this is doing is creating a standard fare (substandard in quality) by reducing alternative voices and products. This leads to tremendous advantages for those seeking to manipulate world opinion.

Unlike Hollywood defenders, I believe that films do have an impact on viewer attitudes and behavior. Research clearly shows that media violence increases children's violent behavior and that sexual content in media dramatically increases sexual activity.[2]

During the furor over the release of "The Last Temptation of Christ," one studio executive arrogantly proclaimed that he didn't care if the public didn't like what they released; they would learn to like it. At least in the golden era of Hollywood, the moguls seemingly tried to entertain the public in responsible ways, which didn't offend. Respect was still a factor in our social climate. Today, reducing the public to an ignorant, immoral mass is being largely achieved through the influences of "pop culture." Prime-time television and music lyrics have become shockingly disgraceful. You can't even peruse the TV guide "menu" channel, without being shocked by the promotional fare. We are expected to believe that this "entertainment" is a reflection of our society and not the "Pied Piper" that it really is.

In contrast to Hollywood's attitude to "The Last Temptation"—and thousands of other genuinely offensive films—Mel Gibson's "The Passion" was rejected by all of the industry distributors. Unlike most independent filmmakers (but fortunately for Mel), he had the personal resources (over $30 million) and a superstar's networking capability to market the film without Hollywood's blessing. Normally, controversy would attract Hollywood interest, but not a Christian film. In the eyes of their community, it was viewed as "anti-Semitic" and not deserving of release. *Entertainment Weekly*, reflecting the interests of its controllers, rated "The Passion" as the most controversial film of all time.[3] However, to the overwhelming Christian community, the film was not an assault on the Jewish community, but a recording of biblical events.

MEL GIBSON

I have respect for Mel, although I'm disappointed that he did not help lead the fight to reclaim an industry for more traditional and positive American representations. I met with his father, Hutton, on a couple of occasions and know that this was of consideration. I pressed with Hutton, but he was not able or willing to convince Mel to resurrect the distribution entity that he had created. It was a compromise by Mel to appease an industry that had helped create him, yet ultimately would try to destroy him. This was a terrible loss for quality independent filmmakers who needed a hero to challenge the industry of its evils.

Hollywood's contempt for other's beliefs even extends to Tom Cruise. His behavior is certainly no more startling than many of Hollywood's other stars, yet he was soundly discredited and thrashed in Hollywood for his denunciations of psychiatry and medication dependencies. Viacom (Paramount) chief Sumner Redstone considered Tom's behavior unacceptable.[4] In typical Hollywood fashion, a few weeks after condemning Tom, Redstone hypocritically lambasted the Federal Communications Commissions for creating a "great deal of fear" among artists.[5] He was responding to fines the FCC imposed on his CBS during their crackdown on indecency. Long term, Mr. Redstone and the other industry moguls will not have to fear fines and can pursue their agendas unfettered. Federal court and commission rulings now define material indecent if it "depicts or describes sexual or excretory activities or organs in a patently offensive manner as measured by contemporary community standards."[6] If community standards disintegrate as much in the next 50 years as they have in the last 50 years, anything will be acceptable.

Talent that will stretch the envelope of decency and perform in the most shocking and vulgar ways are rewarded by Hollywood. Many pop culture icons and today's role models are in need of help, not the attendant publicity and career promotion that Hollywood bestows upon them. What a diversion from the important issues of the day.

Filmmakers such as Quentin Tarantino are embraced by Hollywood and their destructive messages are promoted with incredible fanfare. Dysfunctional "stars" are paraded before us as role models, especially when they come from traditional Christian or European-American backgrounds, but notoriously spurn those values. Lady Gaga and Madonna immediately come to mind.

Madonna's Crucifix stunt.

Regarding what I call "Hollywood's poster children for dysfunction," it is an unfortunate situation that so many talented young people are denied opportunities unless they are willing to compromise their core values. Potential stars must be prepared to fully prostitute themselves to achieve super-stardom. Stars such as Brad Pitt and Tom Cruise have paid a dear price. My wife worked with Brad's mother in the Springfield, MO school district and we got to know Tom's mother while helping with the Marco Island Film Festival. Proud of their sons' successes, it was also evident that they were very concerned about the destructive influences of Hollywood.

I have experienced the motion picture industry paradigms from both a Hollywood/studio perspective and from that of the guerrilla filmmaker. Producing motion pictures does not require spending $50 million-plus, as Hollywood routinely does. Similar quality can be produced for a small fraction of their budgets with a team that knows how to employ cost-effective production techniques and avoid the industry pitfalls.

Surprisingly, Hollywood producers possess an amazing lack of professional expertise and are not known to be inspiring "team players." This requires them to spend vast sums of money catering to the excesses of high-priced personnel. Hollywood notoriously and consistently rejects true talent for their "insider packaging." Due to cronyism and nepotism, audiences are left with role models who do not exude beauty, charisma, or even socially acceptable behavior, but represent the "anti-hero"—whose ignoble ends justify despicable means.

To go up against Hollywood is a daunting task. They will ignore quality independent efforts and set production hurdles and distribution barriers to stop them. I've experienced it all, most devastatingly when trying to play by their rules. I was able to find some work in Hollywood—as an assistant producer/director on low budget independent productions, but never any studio productions. None of the films were good, and there was no money to be made (only the elusive deferred promises), but they were great for experience.

Throughout those years, and since, we met many celebrities at industry events, public outings, or while working on projects, including Robert Redford, Ryan O'Neal, Farrah Fawcett, Leonardo DeCaprio, Vincent Price, Glenn Ford, Robert Wagner, David Hasselhoff, Eric Estrada, Molly Ringwald, Joan Rivers, Rod Steiger, Gil Gerard, Sean Young, Peter Brown, Troy Donahue, Bo Svensen and others. We have interesting stories about many, but for the most part they were kind and considerate, albeit captive of their celebrity. Sadly, it seemed to us, they longed to be ordinary people.

I did get to work with several stars, including Tony Curtis, Isaac Hayes, Denver Pyle, Red Foxx, William Smith, Brad Johnson, and many others . . . and they were great people. Tony Curtis surprisingly called me a couple weeks after winding up a difficult (and for him a "come back") production . . . a classy guy, as were most. Denver was a wonderful man, who surprisingly bought me lunch, twice (at a time when my wallet was getting thin). He reflected hopefully on my generation improving a degenerative industry that he had once cherished.

After many years of struggling in Hollywood and with no success pitching my stories to any of the studios or packaging my own features, we determined to relocate to the Midwest. There I ventured to write, produce, and direct my own feature, "A Place to Grow." It was a subliminal effort to return to my roots and the values that I longed for. The film was a good effort and had potential, but the completion of the film and its release were thwarted by a greed-based company takeover (in the Midwest, no less). Unfortunately, I was not majority stockholder and lost control of the company that I had built, and at the most critical time. Lesson learned: Set up to maintain control!

Sadly, the film, which had an incredible country music soundtrack, was purged of its most powerful scenes, including all of the on-screen singing of its country music star, Gary Morris. Gary was singer of the year in 1983 and had the most amazing voice. He had a relationship with Liberty Records legend Jimmy Bowen, but the soundtrack commitment was abandoned when Garth Brooks had a falling out with Bowen (which unfortunately empowered our takeover team). Subsequently, a Hollywood distribution/sales agent was selected who ignorantly or willfully abandoned the film's intended market (mid-America), and reedited the film to serve totally inappropriate foreign markets... kind of like "The Sound of Music" without music.

On set with Gary Morris and John Beck.

With Wilford Brimley.

Making a motion picture is an exciting process. Over the course of a few weeks' time, many creative people come together and build memories that last a lifetime. John Beck was a gentleman and a blast to work with. Wilford Brimley brought some personal challenges to the production of "A Place to Grow" (the crew didn't appreciate his curmudgeonly attitude), but we got along and, as a great actor, he taught me some excellent directorial lessons. Tracy Kristofferson

With Tracy Kristofferson.

(Kris's daughter) was a sweetheart. On one occasion, when experimenting with a scene, I asked her if she could sing. Her unforgettable response: "Nah, I'm just like my dad."

Other singers in the cast with incredible talent included Juice Newton, Steve Wariner, and Box Car Willie. Box Car, who was an especially good guy (former Air Force and a "hobo") first made his name on "The Gong Show" as an unforgettable train-whistling contestant. He generously gave me a collection of his cassette tapes and wooden train whistle. Box Car was a natural actor, and cousins with Tommy Lee Jones. He told me that he always wanted to be an actor, and that Tommy Lee always wanted to be a singer.

"A Place to Grow" co-writers Woody P. Snow and
Sandy Dillbeck, offering editing advice.

After the company takeover, I met with some other well-known singers and Branson, MO performers about various projects, including Ray Stevens, Jim Stafford, Randy Travis, Ricky Van Shelton and a few others. We met with Brenda Lee and Pat Boone and developed a project about the legendary Red Foley. Unfortunately, after the experience with "A Place to Grow" I wasn't able to attract enough local investment support. The next couple of years were a necessary detour as a media instructor with area colleges. We thereafter moved to Florida, where I felt the opportunities would be greater, and formed

On set with five beautiful ladies.

Black Knight Productions with several West Point friends (West Pointers, at least in sports, are known as the Black Knights).

The Black Knight team was able to secure funds to produce a mystery-western, "Jericho." We produced it in 2000-2001, on schedule and on budget for approximately $870,000. This was remarkable for a period piece with action and a quality cast. At the time, the average budget for a studio production approached $60 million, so we could have made 70 "Jerichos" for that—which should tell you something about Hollywood excess.

"Jericho" starred fellow West Pointer Mark Valley. It was a quality story about the redemption of a man who lost his identity and sought to recapture the love and life of his past. The script was good, but needed improvement, so we did several rewrites, which I believe helped the storyline and characters.

We submitted "Jericho" for major distributor consideration, but most would not even screen it. So we entered it into festivals, thinking that if it did well, distributors would gain an interest. "Jericho" won key awards at three festivals, yet the major distributors still arrogantly ignored us. A couple "bottom feeders" started sniffing around, but they had no money and wanted the standard "license to steal." We decided to test market the film to more mainstream markets and gage audience response. More importantly, we thought that the box office data might be of interest to larger distributors.

"Jericho" poster.

We found theaters to be very responsive to us. They generally dislike the bulk of Hollywood films and appreciate independent competition. Part of the reason is that distributors are always pressuring theaters for the best screens and booking dates, and may withhold a good film, if the theater doesn't accept their "dogs." This gives the distributor leverage over the theaters, making it difficult for an independent to get onto the best screens and especially during the best play dates. We were able to fit into a few cracks and, if we'd had the funds for a large number of release prints and advertising costs, might have been able to roll "Jericho" out to hundreds of theaters across the country. But this was beyond our means.

Before theaters show a film, they want to post the rating for audience members to be guided by. So we submitted "Jericho" to the Motion Picture Association of American (MPAA), which rates films at a fairly substantial cost. The mission of Black Knight Productions was to develop, produce and market quality motion pictures, which promote fresh talent and the best of American ideals. In keeping with that, we were family friendly and believed that "Jericho" would obtain a PG or PG-13 rating. We were shocked when they awarded us an "R" ("Restricted") rating. The film is a mystery-western and has some gunfights, but they are not gratuitous and are motivated out of the story themes of "redemption," "peace over violence," "return to family," and "right over wrong." Ironically, at the same time, several major releases, which, in my opinion, were truly deserving of an "R" rating, were getting "PG" or "PG13." At any rate, the "R" was unacceptable to me and we appealed. The appeals process takes time and money, so I had to temporarily abandon our test market to appear before the appeals board.

It is almost like a court proceeding, where the panel (in our case 14 people), screened the film and then I presented arguments against the "R" rating, while the MPAA presented arguments in support of their rating. Fortunately, the appeals panel was made up of everyday people and the rating was reversed by a vote of 13 to 1. The MPAA representative said that it was unprecedented and that "Jericho" had the distinction of having a rating reversed (without editing changes) by the widest margin in the history of the MPAA. The whole experience led me to conclude that there might exist a dual standard—one for major studio releases and one for select independents. Had we not gotten the rating reversed, our target market would have been significantly reduced. Since then, and with other experiences, documentary director Kirby Dick tackled the MPAA with "This Film Is Not Yet Rated," "on what he charges is one of the most powerful, secretive organizations in the country: the film ratings board."[7]

The MPAA had been formed during the mid-1960s, when President Johnson's speech-writer, Jack Valenti—a media savvy speaker and organizer, would go to Hollywood to become their mouthpiece for self-regulating efforts, thereby abandoning the Hayes Code and its regulations against offensive programming. I'd actually met Mr. Valenti early in 2001, while he critically studied the poster of "Jericho" during a screening that I'd set up for some influential West Point friends at the MPAA's theater in Washington, D.C.. Perhaps our subsequent challenges should not have been surprising. Mr. Valenti was also in Dallas on November 22, 1963, coordinating media activities.

Interestingly, I got a call from Dr. Ted Baehr, of the family friendly "Movieguide," as I left the MPAA appeal's proceeding. He'd immediately heard about our success and congratulated me. His organization considered taking the project under promotional consideration, but ultimately chose not to enter that battleground.

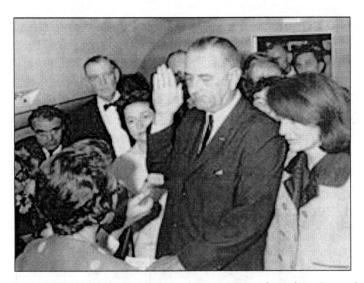

Valenti, seated on left, during Johnson's swearing in aboard Air Force One.

Our test market was fairly successful, especially since we didn't know what we were doing as marketers. In some cases, our box office numbers increased from the first week to the second, which is very unusual unless there is positive word of mouth. Still, our numbers were of no interest to distributors and we had to start swimming with the bottom feeders.

Our only viable distribution support came from Monarch Home Video (a Nashville based independent), which ultimately sold over 70,000 units. Unlike every Hollywood distributor/sales agent that I have ever dealt with, Monarch actually did what they said they would do, and even exceeded expectations. Regards our foreign sales and U.S. cable/television licenses, it is a small network of representatives who can make viable deals. Their loyalty always lies with the buyer (that's their bread and butter) and they view the independent filmmaker as a one-time sucker, in need. As a result, the deals are always one-sided (or they don't happen), and the filmmaker must trust in their representative's performance and honesty—a big mistake. Unfortunately, there is no alternative, unless you have the resources to self-distribute—an increasing difficult prospect. This is but one of the many barriers erected by Hollywood to stifle independent competition.

"Jericho" did eventually air on several Starz channels (most often the Western Channel) and we received positive subscriber feedback, but very little money—thanks to our Hollywood deal structure. Foreign sales were also abysmal. Our Hollywood foreign sales rep didn't secure 5% of the sales revenue that he predicted. When all was said and done, we only got a fraction of our money returned and ultimately sold the film for peanuts to be done with it. There was then one less independent filmmaker and "Jericho" would thereafter belong to a distributor's library, where it might suddenly gain value in the television and other after markets. Ultimately however, although of a classic nature and timeless genre, "Jericho" will probably disappear into oblivion, since it has Christian themes.

Miller Family during "Jericho" production.

In the story, Jericho was rescued by a black preacher named Joshua, played by rodeo/bull fighting legend Leon Coffee. What a great team and great friends Leon and Mark became. Leon kept us all in stitches and Mark kept the ladies attentive. Mark, who could impersonate anyone, would later go on to star as Keen Eddie, The Human Target, and in other prime time series. Mark had great potential and even married the niece of Rupert Murdock, Anna Torv. After their split, Mark's career, not surprisingly, went south.

Other "Jericho" stars included R. Lee Ermey (Full Metal Jacket, and Glock pistols fame), Buck Taylor (of Gunsmoke and many great westerns), and country singers, Lisa Stewart and Mark Collie. Collie played an incredible bad guy, and would pick guitars in the evenings,

With one of my personal heroes, Buck Taylor.

With award winning cinematographer, Jerry Holway, and Jericho's
leading ladies, Morgana Shaw and Lisa Stewart.

while Buck showed other talents as a gifted painter. One of my most
satisfying moments was with R. Lee. A former Marine tough guy
(with a soft heart), he wanted to play the Marshal with a realistic,
but somewhat profane tongue. I convinced him that he didn't need
to, and could deliver this character to family audiences in classic
manner. He took it as a challenge and was incredible. He later
opined, as we sat through the second screening at the World Fest
Houston, "a damn good movie." I am also proud of that film, but
getting it to audiences would prove "a damn good challenge."

R. Lee Ermey, right, after performing his Drill Sergeant routine from "Full Metal Jacket" to "Jericho" teammates, including several "Black Knights."

In trying to secure wide distribution, I learned a most important Lesson: Do not rely on any associations in Hollywood, especially if you are their ideological antithesis. Instead, develop your own marketing and distribution capabilities, as Walt Disney painfully learned three-quarters of a century earlier.

The greatest challenge is developing new distribution models to market motion pictures outside of the Hollywood channels. Create a "name brand" that audiences will come to recognize in anticipation of future quality products. The Internet provides the most revolutionary means to publicize and market projects. Avoid competing against Hollywood and its traditional and very expensive means of distribution. Instead take advantage of a project's unique qualities. With creative advertising campaigns and the promotional assistance of concerned support groups, you might achieve public awareness without spending a fortune for advertising.

For anyone who is not a part of Hollywood's elite, avoid them altogether. This has become better understood since Mel Gibson self-marketed The Passion of the Christ—after Hollywood, motivated by their anti-Christian bias, put up their roadblocks. His surprising success helped to redefine a new and better course of action for independent filmmakers.

Despite our failure to attract Hollywood support for "Jericho", we had surprising support develop within segments of the West Point community, who liked the film and saw the merits of our plans. One of our team, who I'm certain had formerly worked for the CIA, with associates in the Mossad, tried to acquire a greater interest in the company and wanted us to pursue "gung ho" military projects. This took place just before and after 9/11. I even had a couple of my wealthiest classmates express interest in bringing substantial investors into the company to bankroll our growth. There was strong interest in developing a company persona that would enable us to successfully work with Hollywood and be the "go to guys" for advancing pro-military, pro-war projects.

Meetings were to take place, but were strangely cancelled, when I learned about the USS *Liberty* and wanted to instead pursue telling that story. In retrospect, I believe that I was rejecting Black Knight Productions becoming a front company for the CIA (or Mossad). At any rate, the investment interest dissipated quickly during those months following "Jericho" as I continued to research the USS *Liberty*. I believed that I was pursuing a critically important and patriotic story, without fully realizing how politically incorrect and repellent it would be to the moneyed interests.

Somehow Andrew Breitbart heard about my persistent efforts and we met for lunch. He was a dynamo and we hit it off, however he was somewhat coy and evasive with me about my politically-incorrect pursuit and tried to redirect my interests into Christian market films, going so far as to introduce me to a friend. Andrew had just written *Hollywood Interrupted* and was simpatico, but also a realist. Unfortunately, I let the relationship die, but he did send me his book.

Shortly thereafter, we moved to Tennessee and I fell further down the rabbit hole.

In pursuit of truths, I met many politically incorrect people. While seeking support for an independent film project about ancient Germanic hero, Arminius, entitled "The Liberator," I was labeled as having racist associations—to destroy my filming prospects in the historic river town of Herman, MO. This media attack (in the geographic area of our intended filming) was enabled by the SPLC tracking me and employing their insidious influence. They went so far as to incorporate in my Wikipedia biography that I had an "all-white production company"—technically true since I was the only employee. But the implication was that I would not hire minorities. What they failed to mention is that on my previous film project, "Jericho," I had employed several minorities, including the black co-star and the film's Puerto Rican editor. In fact, a main theme of that story, of which I was the principle creator and manager, was opposing discrimination.

I've always tried to hire based on needs and the best available. But this was an example to me of the power these organizations have in controlling public discourse to unfairly smear those who they seek to destroy. I tried, more than once, to correct the several wrong entries in my Wikipedia bio, but within a day or so, they would revert back… no doubt courtesy of these organizations and their monitoring agents, who are probably paid with taxpayer dollars.

I did eventually write "False Flag," about the shocking Israeli attack on the USS *Liberty*, the scandalous cover-up, and how it has impacted our Middle East foreign policy. Had any other nation been the culprit, it would have been made into a major motion picture, probably several times. The story has incredible drama with international implications. It is full of mystery, action, betrayals, and most importantly, individual stories of incredible heroism and sacrifice. The *Liberty* crew has one of the most compelling voices in history and it is unconscionable that it has not been heard in America.

There was, of course, no Hollywood interest, but I persisted in trying to find West Pointers who would see the importance and potential of the project. At one point in time, I scheduled to attend a West Point Society function in south Florida. I had previously been that Society's Secretary and had served on their Board for several years. It was probably the wealthiest society and I looked forward to meetings to advance the project. On the evening of our big Founder's Day dinner, I became violently ill. It prevented me from pursuing the support, and I remained ill for several days. I later determined how I had been poisoned, and by whom, based on the subtext of things said prior and after. I'm sure that it was not an intention to kill, but to send a clear message . . . not just to me, but to those who I was to meet privately the next day.

"False Flag" promotional poster.

Despite the difficulties of producing a motion picture, especially when politically incorrect, it still can and must be done. We need to find and support committed young filmmakers, who are not afraid to tackle difficult truths and chart inspirational and positive courses. Humanity's salvation now requires it.

Over the next few years, my efforts were to become increasingly political.

**CHAPTER NOTES:**

1 *Hollywood vs America*, Michael Medved.

2 "Racy Media Increases Teen Sex, Study Says," Michael Conlon, Reuters, April 3, 2006.

3 *Entertainment Weekly*, June 16, 2006, p. 35.

4 AOL Entertainment News, "Paramount Cuts Ties With Tom Cruise," Aug. 22, 2006 (Reuters).

5 *The Hollywood Reporter*, weekly edition Oct. 17-23, p. 1.

6 *Ibid.*, p. 95.

7 Gregg Goldstein and Anne Thompson, "Filmmaker Lifts Lid on Secretive Ratings System," Reuters, Jan. 23, 2006.

GEORGE WASHINGTON

CHAPTER 20

# The 'Mainstream' Media

"If the freedom of speech be taken away,
then dumb and silent we may be led,
like sheep to the slaughter."
—GEORGE WASHINGTON

⁓✳⁓

The media has consolidated into just a handful of major conglomerates, vertically integrated, controlling everything
from development through production to final distribution, and this power is now directed against their natural
enemies—spiritual, freedom loving, traditionally valued people—
and against sovereign nations. Global elites have an agenda of ultimate control of the masses and to secure it they must destroy people's
values and sense of identity—most importantly, in America. Our
youth are regularly de-
sensitized to violence
and fatalistically condi-
tioned to accept, if not
worship, occult and su-
pernatural powers—and
deny intrinsic attitudes
and beliefs based on
goodness.

As an extremely pow-
erful and influential in-
dustry, the mainstream
media determines pub-

lic discourse and can alter people's beliefs and attitudes. It is also the most discriminatory industry in America—dominated by Jewish interests who serve, wittingly or not, a globalist agenda. The dominance of the "mainstream" media has been very destructive to America, as it restricts discussion of issues critical to our national security and our economic and cultural well-being. Fortunately, like the Gutenberg press in its day, the Internet is a revolutionary new communication medium, offering alternative forms of news, idea exchanges, and entertainment. We must insure that it does not fall under government or special interest control and censorship.

We must become cognizant of the media's leveraged abuses of our public trust and work to create viable opportunities for alternative media. Anti-trust actions should be considered to remove this destructive concentration of power so that other voices can be heard, which might have more positive impacts on our society.

Our enslavement to mass media began approximately 100 years ago. J.P. Morgan and others underwrote a campaign to acquire the 25 most influential newspapers in the country. They brought in their own editors and over the course of the next several years would alter public perceptions away from truthful realities—serving their own nefarious purposes. At about the same time, Edward Bernays, nephew of Sigmund Freud, led efforts to employ crowd psychology throughout the field of mass communications. He became known as the "father of public relations," a euphemism for "propaganda" (for more information, see www.merlinmiller.com/control-media-control-minds/). Unfortunately, as Mark Twain keenly observed, *"It is easier to fool people than to convince them they have been fooled."*

In 1996, President Clinton signed the Telecommunications Act, which has put an incredible number of independents out of business by allowing the major companies to expand their ownership holdings. This is why traditional local programming is disappearing in favor of nationally syndicated programming. As an example of how this restricts competition and silences alternative voices, Clear Channel Communications, as the largest radio group owner, went from 62 stations in 1996 to 1,233 by 2003.[1] Similar consolidations have taken place with television station ownership and with newspaper and magazine publications.

Why should this be upsetting? Not only does it reduce opportunities for media professionals, but it reduces voices of dissent in the media and eliminates a competitive climate which might give the public better entertainment and more truthful news. Mark Cooper, director of research at the Consumer Federation of America, said, "The cornerstone of the FCC's argument to relax ownership limits is that consolidation is in the public interest. The evidence to the contrary is very clear. Stations that consolidate don't produce more news; they produce less. And diversity of news and opinion from the most influential media declines. The record is clear: More consolidation hurts our democracy."[2]

Most outlets now sound alike and share the same messages. Those shows, which purport to offer dissenting viewpoints, are often staged, or unfairly slanted so the audience will accept predetermined conclusions. This channeling "Hegelian dialectic" is a powerful tool for propagandists fulfilling their own agendas. It is amazing how many Americans have been "dumbed-down" through the manipulative and evolutionary processes of mind control. The motion pictures "They Live" and "V for Vendetta" interestingly pay homage to this and have found a cult following by those who are starting to question the obviousness and intent of this mass propagandizing.

As Tom LaHaye questioned in *Mind Siege*, referring to President Clinton: "How could a draft dodger, a womanizer, a pathological liar, and one who, as a college student, demonstrated against his own country in a foreign land, be elected president of a patriotic, moral country? It cannot be explained without acknowledging the power of the media."

In recent years, reporters have been accused and fired from their jobs for falsifying reports. Usually, we find out only when a competitor gets wind of it and it can be proven. Whether television, radio or newspaper reporting, this should be a serious offense. Ratings pressures, however, and a decreasing level of professional ethics with the focus on promoting one's own career or agenda, seem to make it a growing phenomenon. Unfortunately, more and more, the media companies accept it as part of the game. This can go so far as to totally reverse the public's perception of what an event should be. The fact that this happens with growing regularity is quite disturbing.

In this era of digital video and audio production and editing, events can easily be created or altered. An example is when Hillary Clinton was heckled in front of 16 million Americans as they watched the live broadcast of the Concert for New York City on VH1 (a subsidiary of MTV, owned by Redstone's Viacom, which also owns CBS). She walked on stage, apparently to get some political mileage out of honoring the heroes of 9/11. It was a great embarrassment that the police and firemen of NYC booed her on national television.

On Christmas Day, when it re-aired, and when DVDs were marketed of the concert, the videos had been doctored and Hillary walked on stage to great applause and cheers—quite a public relations coup.[3] When the media can have this kind of power to manipulate public opinion to promote their political favorites, then we are heading into Orwell's world.

Hillary Clinton

Interestingly, when presidential candidate Hillary Clinton's prospects for election became questionable in 2008, Senator Barrack Obama, an even more extreme socialist, came out of nowhere with incredible media support to capture the fascination of America. Upon studying his shallow qualifications and controversial positions, it is no surprise that we are experiencing growing civil unrest and an accelerated national decline. The international financiers are making great strides in their bold but systematic moves toward globalism.

As we approach the new election cycle for 2016, the global elites will roll out their new (and old) favorites and create controlled opposition scenarios to misdirect our energies and scrutiny. However, despite these power figures, there is hope for the survival of a free American republic.

The Internet is a phenomenal growth medium that still allows for the free exchange of ideas and is reaching concerned Americans. So far, no one has succeeded in regulating it, although efforts are being made. Unlike other sources of news, items reaching the Internet have not gone through the filter of international news agencies. Today these agencies, with offices around the world, collect, edit, and disseminate news through their valves. As Douglas Reed attested in 1956, "Any hand that can control those valves can control 'the News'—that was not the situation in 1905, nor in 1926, when I became a journalist, but it was developing and today is the situation."[4]

*"To learn who rules over you, simply find out who you are not allowed to criticize."*
—VOLTAIRE

With today's technological capabilities and increasing terrorist security concerns, it is assured that government agencies are eavesdropping on Internet communications. "NSA has managed to find ways to tap into all of these new technologies—including fiber optic cables—and is pulling in more communications than ever."[5] A growing number of Internet service providers stand at the gateway with similar capabilities; therefore, the degree of individual security protection is questionable, at best. In addition, the growing Patriot and Freedom Acts will allow expanding use of these intercepts. If we are not vigilant, the portals of the Internet will allow, in the future, only "approved" news for dissemination, with the monitoring of dissidents.

**CHAPTER NOTES:**

1 *The Hollywood Reporter*, Sept. 19-25, 2006, p. 94.

2 *The Hollywood Reporter*, "Old Media Making Pitch—Firms urge FCC to ease ownership rules in '07," Oct. 24-30, 2006, p. 54.

3 *Hilary's Secret War*, Richard Poe, WND Books, 2004, pp. 5-7.

4 Reed, p. 215.

5 *Body of Secrets*, James Bamford, Anchor Books, April 2002, p. 464.

PATRICK HENRY

# CHAPTER 21

# Who's in Charge

"The Constitution is not an instrument for the government to restrain the people, it is an instrument for the people to restrain the government."—Patrick Henry

In time, despite what may be noble intentions, most politicians lose touch with their constituencies and develop special relationships with lobbyists and government administrators. There are approximately 30,000 lobbyists currently preying on the representatives in Washington, D.C., and nearly 30% of representatives have a spouse or child who currently serves as a lobbyist. They know where their bread is buttered. This loss of true representation for the people needs to change immediately, but only will with diligence and common sense reform.

### TERM LIMITS

All branches of government should be subjected to term limits to insure that elected representatives, and political appointees, remain connected and answerable to constituencies. Longevity breeds privilege and the opportunity and temptation to succumb to the reward trappings of powerful special interests.

"[T]here are more instances of the abridgement of the freedom of the people by gradual and silent encroachments of those in power, than by violent and sudden usurpations."          —James Madison

## CAMPAIGN FINANCE REFORM

The entire political process has been co-opted by money and media. It is not unrealistic to say that elites select our candidates and the media elects them. When comparing campaign contributions, it is quite obvious that establishment candidates are supported by large banks, big business, and media conglomerates while marginalized grassroots candidates must rely on small individual contributors.

"Tea Party" float, Gatlinburg Christmas Parade, 2007.

During Ron Paul's presidential campaign of 2007/2008, we formed a Ron Paul Meetup Group in Sevier County, TN, which quickly came to total 50 dedicated members. After Ron Paul left the race, our burgeoning "Tea Party" was left foundering—with most of us sidelined. Opportunistically, the neocon element of the Republican Party then stepped in to hijack the Tea Party movement . . . beginning with Sarah Palin and evolving to a cacophony of establishment supported yet self-described "grassroots candidates." Most remaining Tea Partiers are frustrated, yet do not fully realize that they are now guided by gatekeepers for Zionist interests, who want Christians pitted against Muslims. This is aggravated by illegal immigration and warmongering.

In 2011/2012, I was recruited to be a presidential candidate for a new independent political party (http://merlinmiller.com/platform-potion/). Impossible prospects for competitive funding simply made it a quixotic adventure. Although grassroots America is searching for true representation, independent voices are prevented from effectively entering the arena. Finance laws allow for super PACs (political action committees) and their controlling billionaires to buy candidates and totally subvert the electoral process.

Finance reform should disempower corporations, labor unions, and businesses from contributing to persons running for federal office and limit individual contributions. In addition, states should be encouraged to reassess their candidacy requirements, allowing the common citizen greater ability to seek local, state, and national office. This should be aided by reducing filing fees, petition requirements, and the length of the campaign season.

## LAWS

Far more laws take effect each year than are eliminated. It has become an unmanageable, non-productive bureaucratic nightmare, especially for small businesses. And hypocritically, many of these laws do not apply to Congress or the executive branch. Also, federal bureaucracies create excessive rules and regulations, which are not only costly but time consuming and invasive to the American people. Many of these bureaucracies and the 47 unelected so-called "czars" should be eliminated. Costly, uncontrolled growth of government is reprehensible, and anathema to the American spirit.

## BENEFITS

All congressional pensions should immediately be terminated. The residual amounts accumulated should be transferred to the Social Security Trust Fund and all congressional members and aides enrolled into the Social Security System. Congressional franking privileges should immediately be terminated. All Congressmen's and their aides' healthcare benefits should be terminated immediately with residual cash benefits transferred to the Medicaid fund. U.S. Air Force travel benefits for congressional members and staffers should be terminated, as the U.S. Air Force should not be a transport service for Congress and the president should not use military transport for campaigning or vacations.

## STATES RIGHTS

The federal legislative, executive, and judicial branches have continuously eroded the power of the states, violating the Tenth Amendment of the Constitution, especially since enactment of the 17th Amendment in 1913. Before passage, state legislative bodies appointed two U.S. senators to represent the state, who were answerable to the state legislatures. The 17th Amendment stripped from the states any influence they had previously enjoyed in the enactment of laws and the protection of their individual sovereignty. Senators have since been elected at large—with special interest money support and media coverage. This has resulted in the continuous erosion of states rights and the massive un-checked expansion of the federal government. We should repeal the 17th Amendment to the Constitution.

Without diligence and strict adherence to the Constitution, a centralization of government power evolves in time. We must work to keep the federal government out of state jurisdictional matters by closely adhering to the Constitution and the 10th and 11th Amendments.

## VOTER FRAUD

The number of incidents of voter fraud is now skyrocketing due to electronic recording and tabulation and gerrymandering. It is relatively simple for hackers and programmers to manipulate the outcome. Soviet dictator Josef Stalin famously said, *"I care not who casts the votes, only about those who count the votes."*

States should consider a return to paper ballots with a check and verification system to insure that voter fraud and tampering does not occur. Also, foreign owned or affiliated companies should never be contracted for voting tabulations.

Well-funded partisan organizations, such as the notorious ACORN, which have been proven to routinely break laws, should never be allowed to influence voter actions and facilitate or impede turnouts. This encourages fraud and intimidation.

Each state has its own ballot access laws, which make it extremely difficult, time consuming and costly for independent parties to qualify. The major parties are able to circumvent many of the requirements (including signature petitions). Unfortunately for new parties, it is generally easier to qualify candidates as independents, rather than on a party slate. The upstart parties are increasingly subject to unfair rules, set by the two dominant political parties.

## THE CONSTITUTION AND JUSTICE

The judiciary is out of control. Recent appointments to the Supreme Court have altered interpretations of the Constitution. Appointments should be subject to term limits. Increasingly, Justices support the misconception of a "Living Constitution," whereby they claim that the Constitution is a "living" document that must be interpreted based on the norms of society at the time, rather than as an uncompromising delineation of rights and responsibilities—the Founders' guideline for good, but limited government.

A grassroots organization, the National Liberty Alliance (NationalLibertyAlliance.org), is working to educate Americans about restoring proper common law grand juries to preserve the rights of the people. Our judicial system has become thoroughly corrupted. Lawyers, judges and the various bar associations have usurped the power of the people, enslaving them with a confusing and convoluted system based on corporate or admiralty law. As a result, injustice is often the outcome of the judicial processes, and our prisons are more overloaded than any other nation in the world. The American people increasingly seek a return of real justice to the land, and protection of our God given rights.

The Justice Department now regularly exceeds its authority and tries to adjudicate matters where it clearly does not have jurisdiction, yet allows criminals in government and banking to break laws without fear of prosecution. At the same time, they attack states for enforcement of constitutional legislation.

To restore our republic, we must have better understanding of the Constitution and Bill of Rights. All three branches of the federal government are in violation of these central governing documents, and it is up to the citizenry to hold government accountable and not allow usurpations which strip us of our rights. Central to understanding America's early success is appreciating the Founders' goal of securing "Life, Liberty, and the pursuit of Happiness"—property rights being essential to the pursuit of happiness.

RON PAUL

# CHAPTER 22

# Marked for Destruction?

"It is no coincidence that the century of total war coincided with the century of central banking."—RON PAUL

A modern-day nation, even a republic such as America, can be destroyed by the carefully coordinated actions of a small but intensely dedicated group of people. Thomas Paine published "Common Sense" in early 1776 to help awaken, unite, and activate the American colonists to shake off the tyranny of England and the international bankers. We live in similar times, fighting the very descendants of these same bankers and their extensive network of enablers.

There are five principal ways that they destroy a nation, and all five are at work in America today.

## FINANCIAL TYRANNY

As Napoleon Bonaparte reflected:

> "When a government is dependent upon bankers for money, they and not the leaders of the government control the situation, since the hand that gives is above the hand that takes. Money has no motherland; financiers are without patriotism and without decency; their sole object is gain."

Poor nations, excepting a small privileged class, do not enable a good quality of life for the overwhelming majority of their people—and they are easily exploited by wealthy nations, international bankers, and multinational corporations. When a government, and by obligation its people, become indebted they are responsible to their creditors. Leverages can then be applied by organizations such as the World Bank, the International Monetary Fund, and the United Nations. Even a nation rich in natural resources can become quite poor. Throughout history, the mercantile pursuit of resources has led to conflicts and on many occasions the impoverishment of innocent people.

A nation like the United States, blessed with an abundance of natural resources, an inspired form of constitutional government, and an ambitious and capable populace, should always be wealthy. However, our own country is now irredeemably indebted and the once strong, defining middle class is being systematically wiped out. Our production capability has been eroded by a political establishment determined to further this economic decline on behalf of the Federal Reserve banking system. This assault is now in its final stages. Only by ousting these criminal leeches and restoring sound money can we recover our production capabilities and restore America's sovereignty.

## MILITARY INTERVENTIONISM

"If my sons did not want wars, there would be none."
—GUTLE SCHNEPER (wife of Mayer Amschel Rothschild)

Wars are costly to a nation's finances and to the lifeblood of its youth. When they are not justified, not constitutionally declared, and not morally conducted, they destroy the heart of a nation, as well as its reputation in the international community. Prolonged wars erode a nation's capabilities for true national defense.

America was disingenuously involved in foreign interventions throughout the 20th century and now into the new century with the so-called War on Terror. If we allow a continuation of this tyrannical spreading of "democracy," and particularly if we fall victim to Israel's deceptions and begin a new war against Iran or Russia, America will inevitably fall. We must be particularly wary of false-flag operations and media lies that manipulate America into further conflicts for the international bankers in their pursuit of global hegemony.

## DEMOGRAPHIC CHAOS

A nation is defined by its people. Race, religion, language, customs, and heritage determine that nation's character and identity. These characteristics are unique and undeniable and carry their own strengths and weaknesses. Throughout history, people have congregated with like people for communication, comfort, production, defense, and other associative reasons. People with similarities have greater success assimilating with one another and achieving common goals. The more marked the differences, the more potential for prejudice, misunderstanding, and conflict. In nature, and without government coercion or media propaganda, people will generally associate in accord with their similarities. Despite ritually repeated claims by the political and pundit class that have been turned into a national motto, diversity is not a nation's strength.

America is currently undergoing radical demographic changes due to unrestrained immigration policies supported by both Democrats and Republicans. These immigrants generally have little in common (race, language, religion, customs, heritage) with the indigenous population—and it is a government's responsibility to protect the interests of its citizens. This is not happening in America and, as a result, unemployment, crime, and discord are growing rampant and the potential for serious civil strife is increasing dramatically. Affirmative action programs are unfairly, destructively, and unconstitutionally pitting groups and individuals against others—causing much resentment. We must immediately stop these assaults on our indigenous population if we are to preserve America's identity and safeguard her future.

## MORAL DEGENERACY

"Humans are seekers of truth in the long run. They
desire the good rather than the evil, even though they
get hypnotized by the latter for long stretches of time."
—NELSON HULTBERG

The moral character of a nation is closely tied to its peoples' religious or spiritual beliefs, its educational foundations, and its cultural norms. Traditionally, individual values are developed within the family unit and reinforced in the community and the larger society, where responsible laws help to enforce good moral behavior.

During the 20th century, organized forces recognized the power of altering our nation's moral character by propagandizing the American people and influencing attitudes and beliefs in a decadent and demoralizing direction.

The undermining of religion, education, and especially the family is now extreme—with political correctness superseding all logic and fairness (an "Alice in Wonderland World"). The "mainstream" media (film, television, music, books, etc.) has been a most useful tool in capturing and distorting the minds of our people, and societal role models have become increasingly amoral. The promotion of sloth, decadence, unethical behavior, sexual perversion, and violence are destroying our youth and any potential for a peaceful and productive society.

## GOVERNMENTAL DYSFUNCTION

*"The most terrifying words in the English language
are: 'I'm from the government and I'm here to help.'"*
—PRESIDENT RONALD REAGAN

When a government becomes corrupt and dysfunctional, its people suffer through disorder, unfair taxation, and loss of liberties and livelihood. The republican form of government can govern well, when it governs less. When government grows beyond its constitutional limits, abuses result and government becomes unanswerable and unaccountable to the people. This centralization of power is particularly destructive to entrepreneurship, individual liberty, and the middle class. Reflecting the elitist attitude of exceptionalism, Henry Kissinger said, "The illegal we do immediately, the unconstitutional takes a little longer."

Today in America, politicians have shredded the Constitution and betrayed their constituencies. As a result, they have deservedly very high disapproval ratings and are generally considered as "owned." As evidenced by the "bailouts," their contempt for working-class Americans and their subservience to special interests is despicable, if not treasonous. Groups such as the Council on Foreign Relations (CFR), the Southern Poverty Law Center (SPLC), the Anti-Defamation League (ADL), and the American Israel Political Action Committee (AIPAC) have abnormal and unhealthy degrees of influence on government servants and the corporate media. This results in discriminatory and partisan behavior and actions that are destructive to our freedoms and traditional American interests.

Each of these five ways to destroy a nation impacts the others with compounding effect, and has roots with global elite machinations beyond the general knowledge or awareness of most Americans.

PAT BUCHANAN

# Chapter 23

# *Let's Have an Un-Party*

"Our two parties have become nothing but
two wings of the same bird of prey."
—PAT BUCHANAN

P at Buchanan is absolutely correct, as he has been with most of his political commentary and thought-provoking books… which is why he has been moved to the sidelines of proper public discourse.

The corruption within both major parties is becoming clear to large numbers of frustrated voters, as they realize that the political machinery exclusively represents special moneyed interests and not their natural constituencies. The question I hear most often by Americans who have awakened to this realization is, "What can we do?"

The answer is really simple—decide to make a difference! As Thomas Jefferson declared, *"I have Sworn upon the Altar of God eternal hostility against every form of tyranny over the mind of man."* We must do the same.

Impossible?

It just requires commitment and action. Walt Disney said, "If you can dream it, you can do it." There are two areas most requiring our effort—media and politics. Media could be creating an alternative web site, or simply informing your neighbor of difficult truths. Politics means holding your representatives accountable to "we the people." Perhaps it means running for local office, or supporting an honorable candidate.

Our goal is to help build a new and vibrant populist political movement/party which will unite American nationalist interests. Existing independent parties need to come together for the common cause of restoring our republic. Isolated, no small party can hope to successfully challenge the Republicans and Democrats. United, as a "nationalist/populist/patriot" coalition, they could!

Ron Paul was the most successful at this, and creation of the "Campaign for Liberty" and "Young Americans for Liberty" provides hope. At one time, Dr. Paul left, but later returned to the Republican Party because he felt that it was the only way to overcome marginalization and have any chance for success. Today, he is aiding his son, Senator Rand Paul, in a potential takeover of the Republican Party, but I do not believe the entrenched forces (which control both major parties) will allow that. As Ron Paul Jr. once explained to me, their father always wanted to take the direct route from point "A" (our troubled place on the political spectrum) to point "B" (where we need to return—in accordance with America's traditional goodness and the doctrines of our Founders). For political and media acceptance, Rand is taking a circuitous route, with the intention of ending up at the same point "B." My fear is that those compromises will lead to misdirects and a compromise of destination, if not character. We must boldly stand for our convictions and let truth and righteousness speak for us, and not play our betrayers' deceit games.

As conditions continue to deteriorate in America, alternatives to the major parties could explode in public popularity. Important issues, which current representatives and pundits avoid, will come to the forefront. Donald Trump is anything but the common man, yet he is resonating with the grassroots over the issues of immigration and our economy. I do not believe he is a self-made man, or even his own man, but the public is being sold that persona. In my opinion, based on his associations and character, he is a "controlled-opposition" experiment designed to test the populist waters, perhaps undermining any true effort to restore our republic. He could also split the Republican Party, setting the stage for Hillary's success (their families are close). Still, Trump may prove to be the best "mainstream" candidate for America's resurrection and that potential could excite the powers-that-be. They cannot totally destroy our sovereign nation—yet—as Putin and others are challenging the existing Rothschild order. If Trump does build upon his "nationalist" popularity and succeed in 2016, we must be careful that the stage for WWIII is not thereafter set. Redirects (and false flags) are no doubt being engineered. In my opinion, Trump is a global elite member with unquestioning support for the Zionist experiment and their ultimate New World Order... not a man of, or for, "we the people."

AMERICAN EAGLE
PARTY

## AMERICAN EAGLE PARTY—
## "WE THE PEOPLE RESTORING OUR REPUBLIC"

The power of government must be reduced and the states' and peoples' rights restored and protected. As a nascent political party, the American Eagle Party (AEP) must tackle the issues most critical to America's wellbeing, and which respect the Constitution and the vision of our Founding Fathers. This will not be a top-down directed effort, but a decentralized uniting for the benefit of grassroots causes and organizations. The American Eagle Party's mission and platform follow:

### MISSION

The mission of the American Eagle Party is to represent "We the People." We reject the current, corrupt political system, which has allowed government to grow in service to special moneyed interests and their lobbies. It is our desire to unite true patriots, populists, and nationalists to restore America's republic, by honoring the Constitution and the unalienable rights of the people. We must courageously unite with a loyalty to future generations.

# PLATFORM

### END THE WARS AND OCCUPATIONS

- America is a republic, not an empire to police the world.
- We have no business intervening in the affairs of other sovereign nations and cannot afford the expenditures. As our Founding Fathers advocated, "Peace, Commerce, and honest friendship with all nations, entangling alliances with none."
- End our foreign military adventures and close most of our overseas bases, redeploying forces stateside.
- Remove any dual citizens from security-sensitive positions in government (including elected office)—America First loyalty!
- Reevaluate our relationship with the United Nations and NATO. Eliminate foreign aid, excepting specifically approved humanitarian relief efforts.

### STOP THE IMMIGRATION INVASION

- Secure OUR nation's borders to protect American interests and preserve our traditions and identity.
- Remove illegal immigrants who have broken our laws and prevent future illegal entry by supplementing our border patrol services with military assistance, as required.

- Revise immigration laws to serve the best interests of the American people, not multinational corporations, international bodies, or foreign interests.
- Make English the official language in the United States and require non-English speakers to gain proficiency before being granted citizenship.

### RECLAIM OUR CONSTITUTIONAL RIGHTS AND LIBERTIES

- Limited government for the people—Freedom, not Tyranny.
- Immediately repeal the Patriot Act, the National Defense Authorization Act (NDAA), and other unconstitutional infringements on the rights of the people (affirmative action, Obamacare, etc.) and return appropriate jurisdiction to the states.
- Reduce government largess by abolishing or restructuring inefficient and invasive departments and agencies.
- Place term limits on federal offices and reform election finance laws to remove the power of special moneyed interests.
- Require Congress to abide by the same requirements which they legislate upon the American people, without exempting themselves.
- Organize town hall meetings to hold political representatives (of all levels) accountable to We the People.
- Repeal acts and executive orders which are in violation of our Constitution and Bill of Rights.

### RESTORE AMERICA'S ECONOMY

- Restore and protect the middle class (traditional transit to a better way of life, which uniquely enabled America to excel).
- End the Federal Reserve System (Fed) and empower the Treasury to issue our currency without interest charge.
- End the IRS and the income tax, replacing with an apportioned tax per the Constitution.
- Balance the federal budget and seek a constitutional amendment to require it.
- Implement policies which empower American workers and entrepreneurs (not multinational corporations and foreign competitors) through fair trade agreements and production incentives.

Renegotiate our so-called "free" trade agreements and establish reasonable but protective tariffs.

• Develop incentives to relocate and grow the domestic production of natural resources, industry, agriculture, and manufacturing.

• End socialist programs which serve to redistribute wealth from the working classes to others, and which negatively impact our values and productivity.

## PROMOTE HEALTHY MINDS AND BODIES

• Enable Media Alternatives—a public inspired with truth and morality can remain free and responsible. Encourage development of media alternatives and take anti-trust action against corporate media cartels to break up their information and entertainment monopoly.

• Return education to local communities (including home schooling options), rather than submitting to invasive, inefficient, and destructive government programs and mandates.

• Protect our environment by stopping major corporate schemes that are destroying the natural purity of our air, water, and land—and poisoning our food supplies.

• End corporate and government suppression of patents and medical treatments, which would free the people to have enabling alternatives for production and health.

## EAGLES NEWS NETWORK (ENN): "WHEREVER TRUTH TAKES US"

"All Truth passes through three stages.
First, it is ridiculed.
Second, it is violently opposed.
Third, it is accepted as being self-evident."
—ARTHUR SCHOPENHAUER (1788-1860)

An important part of building a political party in today's corrupt climate requires bringing critical truths to "We the People." We are determined to build our own media channel—the go-to place for accurate political news.

The Eagles News Network will grow into a virtual web channel, posting key articles, news interviews and documentary programs from foreign and domestic sources (including in-house productions) to be a viable alternative to the controlled, propagandistic "Mainstream Media."

Washington crossing the Delaware.

## VETERANS LEAGUE OF HONOR

As an adjunct to our Party effort, we look to form the "Veterans League of Honor" and invite all veterans to help us lead the way back to humanitarian greatness while constitutionally protecting America's vital interests.

See www.AmericanEagleParty.com for more information, or to join our Party effort.

TEDDY ROOSEVELT

# CHAPTER 24

# Summary

"The credit belongs to the man who is actually in the arena; whose face is marred by dust and sweat and blood; who strives valiantly; who errs and comes short again and again; who knows the great enthusiasms, the great devotions, and spends himself in a worthy cause; who at the best knows in the end the triumph of high achievement, and who at the worst, if he fails, at least fails while daring greatly, so that his place shall never be with those cold and timid souls who know neither victory nor defeat."     —TEDDY ROOSEVELT

## CORRECTING OUR COURSE

America can be saved from its current destructive course. It is a country blessed like no other and we have always found ways to overcome. However, it will take heroes committed to the ideals of our Founding Fathers to restore the republic. We are in a spiritual battle for the hearts and minds of the American people, and the outcome will affect the rest of humanity. The New World Order, an elitist concept for controlling world populations, is the enemy to self-determination and national sovereignty. America is still the country most depended upon, by people around the world, for a future of hope and freedom. Over the last century we have let them down, as internationalists have subverted the prospects for peace and prosperity. Let us now do our duty, as our Founding Fathers did before us.

## THE JEWISH QUESTION

In America, better than any other previous host nation, Jews have found the ability to assimilate and prosper. Unfortunately, throughout history, they have been used by internationalists and elements of their own community. According to Albert Einstein, "anti-Semitism is nothing but the antagonistic attitude produced in the non-Jew by the Jewish groups. The Jewish group has thrived on oppression and on the antagonism it has forever met in the world—the root cause is their use of enemies they create to keep solidarity."[1]

Most gentiles are familiar with the overwhelming body of media on Jewish persecutions. However, "if we consult Jewish literature we ascertain that it is this idea of world hegemony which haunts the minds of the Chosen People and impregnates their thoughts and their acts."[2] An ambitious people can easily be acceptant of a mindset of supremacism, especially when it is a part of their heritage and indoctrination, and they experience material benefit by it. The majority of Jewish people are highly intelligent and humanitarian. It is time for them to oppose the would-be "world rulers," the financial barons who have plotted throughout the ages, hijacking the Jewish community for their own purposes. These world puppeteers have been using Zionism to ride the back of the Jewish community like a parasite, feeding off of it and surreptitiously guiding it to eventual ruin. Can Jewish-Americans put America before "tribal" loyalty? Time will tell, but much depends on it.

## RESTORING THE REPUBLIC

As American patriots awaken to combat this evil, we should always keep in mind that it is orchestrated by global elites (the international banking community and their beneficiaries and puppets) and not by the nations, groups or individuals which have been set up as their fall guys—through disinformation and false-flag events. We must recognize where the evil really lies and go after the head of the snake.

We must also be careful that internationalists do not spin this planned New World Order into a less obtrusive, but still collectivist,

The battle at Lexington.

World Order. As more people awaken to the global competition for control, redirects will certainly be planned. It seems to me that two competing factions are now warring for control. The traditional, and, in my opinion, evil Rothschild network versus a growing utopian alternative. In essence, good vs. evil ... but with a caveat... both are forms of collectivism (a euphemism for communism/corporatism). And what may be good for most is not good for all. This is part of the distinction between a democracy (rule of the majority) and a republic (which protects the rights of the individual).

Our Founding Fathers recognized the value of a decentralization of power, self-reliance, and nationalism—rather than any form of socialist internationalism (even when utopian). The more power is concentrated, the greater the potential for abuse. How much power should the collective have in relation to the individual? This is a big part of the challenge that faced our Founders, and that still plagues responsible leaders. Perhaps the greatest resource for understanding the guiding principles of our republic is *The 5,000 Year Leap: A Miracle That Changed the World* by W. Cleon Skousen. In my opinion, it should be required reading for all Americans.

Another critically important book for understanding the outright fraud perpetrated against the American people is *You Know Something Is Wrong When . . .* (Subtitle: *An American Affidavit of Probable Cause*) by Anna Maria Riezinger and James Clinton Belcher. This book lays out how international bankers, through subversive actions and deceitful legalese, have created *de facto* corporate governments, contractually enslaving the people without their knowledge or consent, denying common law and natural rights, and stealing their inheritance.

The battle to restore and protect our freedoms can be fought without violence, but must be fought on many fronts, through peaceful, civil action. The best way for America to get positive change is by replacing the Republicrats with honest, grassroots patriots and doggedly pursuing justice at all levels of government, especially at the federal level. Our primary purpose must be to return our republic back to the constitutional principles of limited government and individual freedom that our forefathers laid out and fought for.

## IN CONCLUSION

As I began this journey by researching the USS *Liberty*, never did I believe that it would take me through such troubling discoveries. I was not a "conspiracy theorist" and although I held certain resentments to the controlled Hollywood establishment, I was not, and am not, "anti-Jewish" or "anti-Semitic." I am, however, very pro-American and resolute in combating discrimination in all forms, including Zionist favoritism and pressure tactics.

Our nation is the greatest ever built and has the incredible potential to truly lead the world to peace and prosperity by being a fair and just role model. However, the United States should not encourage the creation of a "New World Order." The very concept is un-American and implies universal control. We must respect the sovereignty of other nations, and resist all efforts that would destroy our traditions, values and freedoms.

We need to be aware of the five ways to destroy a nation that have been at work for decades, to overcome the global organizers of our destruction. To succeed we must end all unconstitutional wars and ensure that we are not coerced into war against Iran or Russia through false-flag events or lies. We must restore a healthy economy for our people with a sound currency and the enabling of domestic production, so that the middle class can survive as a unique transit to wealth and happiness. We must stop the immigration invasion and secure our borders to restore America's sovereignty and our traditional identity. We need to reawaken the inherent goodness of the American people by honoring spiritual, physical, economic, and social morality. And lastly, we need to restore our constitutional republic, and through our never-ending vigilance, forever maintain it.

The key to our success in each of these areas is dependent upon the pursuit of truth. As Thomas Jefferson said, "Knowledge is power . . . knowledge is safety . . . knowledge is happiness."

As concerned citizens, we should immediately consider these important actions:

- End our foreign military adventures and close most of our overseas bases, redeploying forces stateside.
- Secure our nation's borders, preventing the entry of illegal immigrants, supplementing our border patrol services with military assistance, as required.
- Support and vote for candidates who represent the best of American ideals and will uphold our Constitution and Bill of Rights.
- Reform immigration laws to reduce the invasion and qualify applicants for American citizenship (hold employers accountable and no amnesties).
- Dissolve the IRS and replace it with a simple and fair consumption tax.
- Remove control of money from the Federal Reserve System, repudiating the interest debt, and return the issuance authority to the U.S. Treasury.
- Balance the federal budget and seek a constitutional amendment to require it.
- Reduce government largess by abolishing unnecessary departments (Education, Energy, Labor, HUD, Homeland Security, FDA, Agriculture) and eliminating the "czars" and their staffs. End divisive and un-constitutional affirmative action programs.
- Reduce the size and complexity of government and decentralize government activities to the most local level possible.
- Repeal unconstitutional laws (Patriot/Freedom Act, NDAA,

affirmative action, Obamacare) and return appropriate jurisdiction to the states.

- Reevaluate our involvement with the United Nations and NATO. Work fairly in seeking a just peace in the Middle East, which includes a homeland and self-determination for Palestinians.

- Eliminate foreign aid.

- Renegotiate our trade agreements/treaties (GATT, NAFTA, CAFTA, WTO) to make them "fair" rather than "free" and establish reasonable but protective tariffs.

- Make English the official language in the United States and require non-English speakers to gain proficiency before being granted citizenship.

- Remove any dual citizens from security-sensitive positions in government.

- Commission a thorough investigation of the events of 9/11 to bring the real perpetrators to justice and end the perpetual, Orwellian "War on Terror."

- Place term limits on federal offices and reform election finance laws to remove the numerous advantages of special interests and lobbies.

- Increase the number of congressional representatives, so that constituencies are better served.

- Remove the power of special interest groups and their financial leverage over political candidates.

- Repeal the 14th Amendment and restore to the people and states their sovereignty.

- Repeal the 16th Amendment and cease federal encroachments on states' rights.

- Repeal the 17th Amendment and restore to the states their right to select senatorial representatives.

- Encourage development of media alternatives and take anti-trust action against the established corporate media cartels to break up their information and entertainment monopoly.

- Develop incentives to relocate and grow the domestic production of natural resources, industry, agriculture, and manufacturing.

With these first steps, I believe America would be back on its feet within a short period of time and the American Dream would be restored—so that we would once again be emulated by the rest of the world, rather than despised. In this way, we might leave a world of peace, prosperity, and happiness for our progeny.

I encourage all Americans to shake off any conditioned apathy and get politically active. *We can make the difference!* As Gandhi said, "When the people lead, the leaders will follow." I'm hopeful that many of you will see the benefits of joining the American Eagle Party, and help take back our country!

For additional information or to contact me, please check out "Where Eagles Gather" at www.MerlinMiller.com

May God bless you—and may you always fly with eagles.

**CHAPTER NOTES:**
1 Albert Einstein, *Collier's Magazine*, November 26, 1938.
2 *Freemasonry and Judaism*, Vicomte Leon De Poncins, A & B Publishers, p. 221.

THE CADET CHAPEL AT WEST POINT

# The Cadet Prayer

O God, our Father, Thou Searcher of human hearts, help us to draw near to Thee in sincerity and truth. May our religion be filled with gladness and may our worship of Thee be natural.

Strengthen and increase our admiration for honest dealing and clean thinking, and suffer not our hatred of hypocrisy and pretense ever to diminish. Encourage us in our endeavor to live above the common level of life. Make us to choose the harder right instead of the easier wrong, and never to be content with a half-truth when the whole can be won. Endow us with courage that is born of loyalty to all that is noble and worthy, that scorns to compromise with vice and injustice and knows no fear when truth and right are in jeopardy. Guard us against flippancy and irreverence in the sacred things of life. Grant us new ties of friendship and new opportunities of service. Kindle our hearts in fellowship with those of a cheerful countenance, and soften our hearts with sympathy for those who sorrow and suffer. Help us to maintain the honor of the Corps untarnished and unsullied and to show forth in our lives the ideals of West Point in doing our duty to Thee and to our Country. All of which we ask in the name of the Great Friend and Master of all.

*—Amen*

## NEW SUBSCRIBER SPECIAL:

# American Free Press
## Special Subscription Deal

T here is no other paper in America like *American Free Press* (AFP). Every week the hard-driving journalists at *American Free Press* dig for the truth—no matter where the facts may lead. AFP's reporting has been lauded by prominent personalities across the globe, while here at home the controlled media and global power elite try their best to make you believe what you are getting in mainstream publications and on the nightly news is "the whole truth." Nothing could be further from reality! From the unanswered questions about 9-11, the free trade fiasco, the happenings in our corrupt Congress, uncontrolled immigration, to alternative health news and more, AFP tackles the toughest issues of the day with a candid and provocative reporting style that has earned us a host of devoted followers—and powerful enemies. Isn't it time you started getting a fresh, honest approach to the news that can make or break the future of you and your family?

You'll find all that in AFP plus lots more. AFP is guaranteed to provide all the "sizzle" we promise or we will refund the unused portion of your subscription—no questions asked!

## Special "FREE BOOKS" Offer!

Get a FREE copy of Victor Thorn's *Frontman: Barack Obama Exposed* ($20 retail) when you subscribe to AFP for ONE year (52 issues per year). Get TWO FREE BOOKS—*Frontman* PLUS *Hillary & Bill: The Murder Volume* ($30 retail)—when you subscribe to AFP for TWO years (104 issues) for $89. That's $50 in FREE gifts! Send payment to AFP, 16000 Trade Zone Avenue, Unit 406, Upper Marlboro, MD 20774. Call AFP toll free at 1-888-699-NEWS (6397) to charge. See other subscription offers at www.AmericanFreePress.net.

## AMERICAN FREE PRESS ORDERING COUPON

| Item# | Description/Title | Qty | Cost Ea. | Total |
|-------|-------------------|-----|----------|-------|
|       |                   |     |          |       |
|       |                   |     |          |       |
|       |                   |     |          |       |
|       |                   |     |          |       |
|       |                   |     |          |       |
|       |                   |     |          |       |
|       |                   |     |          |       |
|       |                   |     |          |       |
| | | | SUBTOTAL | |
| | | | Add S&H on books* | |
| | | Send me a 1-year USA subscription to AFP for $49 | | |
| | | Send me a 2-year USA subscription to AFP for $89 | | |
| | | | TOTAL | |

**\*S&H ON BOOKS:** Add $4 S&H on orders up to $25. Add $6 S&H on orders from $25.01 to $50. Add $8 S&H on orders from $50.01 to $75. Add $10 flat S&H on orders over $100. Note: Outside the U.S. email shop@AmericanFreePress.net for S&H. You may also subscribe to AFP or buy books at www.AmericanFreePress.net

**PAYMENT OPTIONS:** ❑ CHECK/MO  ❑ VISA  ❑ MC  ❑ DISCOVER  ❑ AMEX

Card # _____

Expiration Date _____  Signature _____

EAG16

**CUSTOMER INFORMATION:**

NAME _____

ADDRESS _____

CITY/STATE/ZIP _____

**RETURN WITH PAYMENT TO:** AMERICAN FREE PRESS, 16000 Trade Zone Avenue, Unit 406, Upper Marlboro, MD 20774. Call 1-888-699-6397 toll free to charge.

CPSIA information can be obtained
at www.ICGtesting.com
Printed in the USA
FFOW04n0607250416
23429FF